'A powerful challenge.'
John Stott, Rector Emeritus, All S

'This challenging and ground-breaking book really gets under the skin of the reader. Using St Paul's second letter to the Corinthians as his microscope, Jonathan Lamb examines the disciplines and priorities for consistently living a life of Christian integrity. This is applied theology at its most readable – and most demanding.'
Jonathan Aitken, author, broadcaster and former Cabinet Minister

'Whilst admitting the truth that we are all flawed and sometimes fail, Jonathan Lamb calls us to God's uncompromising standards of trustworthiness, service and accountability. This courageous and thorough book encourages everyone to be authentic and depend on God. Everyone is a leader in some area, and nothing is more critical in a leader than integrity.'
Paul Valler, former Finance and Operations Director, Hewlett-Packard Ltd

'We know that God is watching, but so are wives! Keeping up appearances is relatively easy, but who we are at home is a truer reflection of reality. In thirty years of marriage, Jonathan and I know each other's weaknesses but share a determination, by God's grace, to live the life. But perhaps you should talk to our children!'
Margaret Lamb

The author's royalties have been irrevocably assigned to Langham Preaching, a programme of the Langham Partnership International (LPI). Langham Preaching seeks to encourage a new generation of preachers and teachers through the development of preaching movements in countries of the Majority World, providing practical training and support for pastors, lay preachers and evangelists. For further information on the three LPI programmes, please visit the website at http://www.langhampartnership.org.

Jonathan Lamb

INTEGRITY
Leading with God watching

INTER-VARSITY PRESS
Norton Street, Nottingham NG7 3HR, England
Email: ivp@ivpbooks.com
Website: www.ivpbooks.com

First published 2006
Reprinted 2007, 2009

British Library Cataloguing in Publication Data
A catalogue record for this book is available from the British Library.

ISBN 978–1–84474–160–1

Set in Dante 10.5/13pt
Typeset in Great Britain by CRB Associates, Reepham Norfolk
Printed and bound by Ashford Colour Press Ltd, Gosport, Hampshire

Inter-Varsity Press publishes Christian books that are true to the Bible and that communicate the gospel, develop discipleship and strengthen the church for its mission in the world.

Inter-Varsity Press is closely linked with the Universities and Colleges Christian Fellowship, a student movement connecting Christian Unions in universities and colleges throughout Great Britain, and a member movement of the International Fellowship of Evangelical Students. Website: *www.uccf.org.uk*

With gratitude for the example of

George Lamb
Ralph Annear
Philip Levermore
Ben Taylor
John R. W. Stott

Contents

E. Integrity as a way of life

Acknowledgments

Writing a book of this nature has been a challenging experience, for I have at times felt the heat of the battle. This has not just been in relation to the demands of family life and Christian ministry, but in relation to the subject matter itself. I have become more fully aware of the seriousness of the call to consistent Christian living, particularly for those who seek to teach others. 'Not many of you should presume to be teachers, my brothers, because you know that we who teach will be judged more strictly,' says James (Jas 3:1). He continues by saying that 'we all stumble in many ways', and I have been very aware of my need of God's grace and the help of good friends as I have worked away at this subject in the midst of various struggles and temptations.

I therefore gratefully acknowledge the help of so many people who have expressed prayerful solidarity and practical support. I must highlight the devotion of my wife Margaret, who has not only worked tirelessly in support of our shared life and ministry but, through a wonderful combination of Cumbrian forthrightness and Christian grace, has been a constant encouragement to live consistently. Her support, forgiveness and trust have been essential elements in my work at home and beyond. I am also indebted to a wide team of faithful prayer partners, to friends and colleagues in a ministry advisory group which has given wise support, and two friends, Peter Comont and Paul Johnson, with whom I have been able to pray from time to time in the context of open and supportive friendship. Children also have a God-given ability to expose inconsistency and hypocrisy, and I acknowledge with gratitude the help I have received, accompanied by such warmth and good humour, from our three daughters, Catherine, Rebecca and Anna.

I began reflecting on the theme of this book when I was asked by Dan Denk to give a series of lectures at the global consultation of General Secretaries of the International Fellowship of Evangelical Students, held in the Netherlands in 2003. I worked on the material still further following an invitation from Dr Peter Adam to teach at a ministry conference at Ridley College, Melbourne, in 2005. I am grateful for the insights of these audiences, which have sharpened my thinking and application.

I am particularly grateful for the patience of a series of IVP editors, including Eleanor Trotter and Stephanie Heald, who have encouraged within me the gift of perseverance! A number of writers have made a great difference to my understanding of 2 Corinthians, both in the preparation of the Crossway Bible Guide (*Discovering 2 Corinthians*) and in my work on this present title. Inevitably their ideas have informed my writing and, if I have failed to acknowledge that appropriately within the text, I gladly highlight the titles and have listed them in the section 'For further reading' towards the end of the book.

I would also like to express my thanks to Rev. Dr John Stott for his foreword to this volume. I am indebted to him both for the wisdom and clarity of his writing and preaching, and for the godly example of integrity and humility for which he is known around the world. I am glad to name him, and four other men who have also served me as such good examples, by way of a simple dedication at the front of the book.

Jonathan Lamb
Oxford, 2006

Foreword

Integrity, consistency, sincerity, honesty, transparency, authenticity and reliability: what a beautiful cluster of Christian virtues! And what a tragedy that they do not always characterize the people of God!

Yet my friend and colleague Jonathan Lamb goes in search of them in his skilful analytical study of the apostle Paul's second letter to the Corinthians.

Integrity is the quality of integrated persons, in whom there is no dichotomy between their public and their private lives, between what they profess and what they practise, between their words and their deeds. It is an indispensable quality of leaders, and not least of evangelists. As John Poulton (former Archbishops' advisor on evangelism) wrote:

> The most effective witness comes from those who embody the things they are saying. They *are* their message. Christians need to look like what they are talking about . . . What communicates now is basically personal authenticity.[1]

But Jonathan Lamb goes further than challenge us to integrity of lifestyle; he also points the way by reminding us that we are accountable to God who watches, sees, cares and judges.

John Stott
12 June 2006

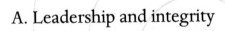

A. Leadership and integrity

1. Why integrity matters

The London *Times* recently carried a small item of news that, surprisingly, had hit the international papers. It was the rather distressing story of a lorry driver who had lost his job. The reason? He drove supply lorries for Coca-Cola, but insisted on drinking cans of Pepsi at work. So he was fired. A little unjust, you might think. Of course, if he had been the chief executive caught with a six-pack of Pepsi under his desk, that would have been another matter. These days, in the new styles of business management, consistency matters. Charles Handy, the business guru, lists as one of his six guiding principles for managers, 'The leader must live the vision.' He must not only craft his mission or vision statement, he must embody it.

We feel much the same about politicians. We are suspicious of manifesto pledges and political programmes at the best of times, but when there is no genuine change in the real world we become cynical about the entire process. Many politicians are undermined by the public's perception of spin, or corruption, or a lack of integrity. We know the stories, since they appear in our newspapers most weeks: deputy prime ministers who betray their wives by having secret affairs with diary secretaries; prime ministers who allegedly sell honours to wealthy donors to their political party; opposition MPs who portray an image of happily married family men, but who cover up their gay relationships; and even a politician who parades his green credentials by cycling to work, while his flunkey drives a limo at a discreet distance behind him, carrying his shoes and briefcase (charged by the papers with being an 'environmental hypocrite'). We could go on.

It is no wonder that the newspapers devote a great deal of newsprint not only to fallen politicians, but also to stories of vicars who embezzle church funds or who run off with the church secretary. Stories like that sell because they are blatant examples of hypocrisy. There is a salacious side to them too, but there is an understandable reaction from the man in the street when he sniffs religious humbug or double standards, particularly coming from priests or politicians who feel they have the right to tell others how they should live.

As Christian believers we know we must set our own house in order. We are too familiar with the high-profile casualties amongst church leaders. We fear that the way we live gives the lie to what we preach. A recent study by the Princeton Religion Research Center demonstrated that, alongside some increase in church attendance in the USA over the last ten years, there was a marked decline in professing Christians who thought there was any connection between Christianity and morality. As one writer expresses it, 'Much of American Christianity is returning to raw paganism: the ordinary pagan can be ever so religious without any necessary entailment in ethics, morality, self-sacrifice or integrity.'[1] Surveys find little difference when comparing the behaviour of born-again Christians before and after their conversion experience. 'In three major categories – use of illegal drugs, driving while intoxicated, and marital infidelity – behavior actually deteriorates after a commitment to Christ ... Recent surveys also indicate that the incidence of divorce is actually higher among those identifying themselves as evangelical Christians than among the general population.'[2] While the statistics might be more readily available in the US, the trends are likely to be global. In my own culture we know all too well the damage caused by the inconsistency of pastors and leaders who call others to live by God's standards yet themselves live a lie. We know they let the side down.

Yet we know our own hearts too. I found it painful to write that last paragraph, for we know the harm done to individuals, families and communities, and most of all the harm done to the name of Christ. It is also painful because we see the evidence of inconsistency in our own lives. All of us know how vulnerable we are in our Christian service, taking responsibility for the well-being of others, teaching them God's ways, known in our workplace as a committed Christian, while at the same time struggling with secret failures and inconsistencies. In Mark Greene's research for the London Institute for Contemporary Christianity, 'maintaining Christian integrity' came a close second to 'stress' in the top five issues facing Christians in the workplace.

Watch your life

The repeated call of Scripture is to live a life worthy of our calling. As John wrote in his first epistle, 'Whoever claims to live in him must walk as Jesus did' (1 John 2:6). It is a matter of faith that works, of truth in action, of godliness in working clothes. The early Christians, of course, could not afford to live inconsistently. As we read the New Testament we see that there is a close connection between holiness and mission. The early church was being watched. Their lives, their work, their families, their values, their response under pressure – all of these had to support their radical message in the first century.

Paul was also acutely aware of the danger facing Christian leaders. When he spoke to the Ephesian elders he stressed, 'Keep watch over yourselves and all the flock of which the Holy Spirit has made you overseers' (Acts 20:28). He said the same to Timothy: 'Don't let anyone look down on you because you are young, but set an example for the believers in speech, in life, in love, in faith and in purity ... Watch your life and doctrine closely' (1 Tim. 4:12, 16). The order is significant in both exhortations: watch yourselves, watch your life, your godliness, your spiritual well-being, first.

Indeed, Paul was fearful of the potential danger of helping others but himself facing shipwreck (1 Cor. 9:27) and engaged in demanding self-discipline so as to avoid being 'disqualified for the prize'. There is a seriousness about Paul's writing, not least because of the special temptations which leaders face. Calvin, the great Reformer and pastor, said that it was a basic strategy of Satan 'to seek some misconduct on the part of ministers which may tend to the dishonour of the gospel'.

The call for integrity

At all levels of society there is a strong appeal for integrity, whether on the part of business, political or religious leaders. It is seen as a fundamental and essential quality of leadership. We should not be surprised to see that it is a high value within the corporate sector. In his book *Transforming Leadership*, Richard Higginson lists some of the mission statements of well-known companies:

- 'Integrity is never compromised. The conduct of our company world-wide must be pursued in a manner that is socially responsible and commands respect for its integrity and for its positive contributions to society.' (Ford Motors)
- 'Shell companies insist on honesty and integrity in all aspects of the business.'
- 'We conduct our business with uncompromising integrity. People at every level are expected to adhere to the highest standards of business ethics and must understand that anything less is totally unacceptable.' (Hewlett Packard)[3]

Integrity features highly amongst employees' concerns too. Business research has shown that, when asked about what they most admire in leaders, integrity is one of the three most cited characteristics. For most employees it means being honest; they want the boss to be straight with people. It also means being consistent. Business leaders or politicians or priests should not say one thing one day and something radically different the next.

In a chapter on integrity for the book *The Seven Heavenly Virtues of Leadership*, Margaret Thorsborne reports on a survey carried out amongst a range of people, including CEOs, middle and senior managers, and staff and their families in organizations of all sizes in Queensland, Australia. When asked to describe the people they would identify as possessing integrity, these are the words the respondents used:

- strength of character;
- steadfast, resolute, having fibre;
- walking the talk, doing what was promised;
- authentic, straightforward, what's on the inside is displayed on the outside;
- open, honest and direct in their dealings with others;
- clear and uncompromised values, and clarity about what's right and wrong;
- committed, with the courage of their convictions;
- behaviour matched values;
- principled, honourable, fair, accountable and responsible;
- balanced, integrated, whole;
- self-aware and self-reflective;
- mature and wise.

But a telling feature of her research was that her respondents could only name a handful of people whom they believed 'had the goods'. By contrast, they had no difficulty in recalling instances when integrity was absent. Her work indicated that, in any community which lacks integrity, the greatest tragedy is the loss of trust.[4] This is bad news for companies, of course, who like to be trusted. They want customers to be confident that the product does exactly what it says on the tin. And they realize that integrity is essential if the organization is to function as it should. Trust is essential in all communities, as we shall see in chapter 7.

The nature of integrity

On the one hand, integrity can mean a state of wholeness, of completeness. In an earthquake zone a block of flats will be checked for structural integrity to ensure that all the pieces still fit together exactly as they are supposed to. One definition of the word 'integral' is 'essential or necessary for completeness; a whole; complete; perfect; uninjured; entire'. In that sense, integrity suggests a life that is well integrated. There is a coherence between the different parts of a person's life. The value system that we profess shapes every area of our lives, public and private. There is a togetherness about our personality and way of life. The Old Testament uses the word *shalom* as an expression for the whole of life having this quality of consistency and harmony, and so some writers suggest that 'integrity' could almost be an alternative rendering.

But integrity has a second related meaning that is more common in everyday conversation. We use it to describe soundness in terms of truth and morality. Integrity means we are upright, honest and sincere. We can be trusted because there is a consistency of word, character and action. This is the outward expression of inward integrity.

In the early pages of the Old Testament, as God's covenant with his people is reaffirmed, the Lord calls Abram to live in a way which corresponds with the wonder of that special relationship. 'When Abram was ninety-one years old, the LORD appeared to him and said, "I am God Almighty; *walk before me and be blameless*. I will confirm my covenant between me and you and will greatly increase your numbers"' (Genesis 17:1–2, my italics).

- First, the Lord calls him to be 'blameless', a word meaning 'whole' or 'integrated'. Abram and all of God's people are to live wholeheartedly for God and sustain their commitment to him with complete integrity. When the same Hebrew word is used to describe animals it is translated 'without blemish'. For God's people, chosen by God Almighty, it is a call to holiness and devotion to him in every area of life.

- Second, Abram is to live with integrity 'before' the Lord. To live before him is to live in his presence. There is nothing to hide, for nothing *can* be hidden in God's presence. It is life lived with God watching.
- Third, it is not achieved instantaneously. It is a call to 'walk before me and be blameless'. It is a lifelong commitment, a consistent manner of life throughout the long pilgrimage of God's people.

The verse embodies the themes with which we are concerned in this book. As God's people, there should be an obvious correspondence between our calling and our lifestyle. He has chosen us and brought us into his family, and we are to display the family likeness, to live lives worthy of our calling.[5] Such a life must be 'blameless', a life of moral integrity and wholehearted devotion. It is the kind of life described in David's prayer: 'I know, my God, that you test the heart and are pleased with integrity ... O LORD, God of our fathers Abraham, Isaac and Israel, keep this desire in the hearts of your people for ever, and keep their hearts loyal to you' (1 Chr. 29:17, 18). Both Old Testament texts underline the environment in which we live. In Genesis 17 it is 'before him'; in 1 Chronicles 29 it is before God who 'tests the heart'. Integrity is living blamelessly with God watching.

A life in sync

Integrity, then, means a coherence in every area of life. Perhaps you have watched a news report on television where the sound and pictures are 'out of sync'. It is hard to take it seriously, as we try to match what is being said with the animated face on the screen. This is what destroys a leader's credibility. When leaders' lives fail to match up with their words, we give up listening. We cannot take them seriously.

In his book *Leadership Jazz*, Max DePree, a Christian who has worked in the higher levels of the corporate sector, writes about his granddaughter Zoe.

She was born prematurely and weighed one pound, seven ounces, so small that my wedding ring could slide up her arm to her shoulder. The neonatologist who first examined her told us that she had a 5 to 10 per cent chance of living three days ... To complicate matters, Zoe's biological father had jumped ship the month before Zoe was born. Realising this, a wise and caring nurse named Ruth gave me my instructions: 'For the next several months, at least, you're the surrogate father. I want you to come to the hospital every day to visit Zoe, and when you come, I would like you to rub her body and her legs and her arms with the tip of your finger. While you're caressing her, you should tell her over and over again how much you love her, because she has to be able to connect your voice to your touch.'

He then draws the lesson for all leaders: 'At the core of becoming a leader is the need always to connect one's voice and one's touch.'[6]

When leaders at any level fail to live with integrity, the fallout is deadly serious. It poisons the community, destroys trust, torpedoes a coherent and unified mission and, most seriously of all, betrays the cause of Christ's gospel and dishonours the God whom we serve. But when Christian leaders live their words, keep their promises, serve their community – in short, show us Jesus Christ – then Christian community is built and Christian mission is enhanced. We know from our own experience that almost everyone respects and admires integrity when they see it. We can have no hesitation in asserting that this one quality, truly understood and faithfully exercised, can transform the work of leaders, strengthen the work of churches and organizations, and support our Christian witness. This is why I feel so passionate about it, and why I long that I should do better.

But let me be clear. While I might be seen as a respected leader and faithful church member, I know my capacity to deceive myself and others. I am acutely aware of my struggles with inconsistent Christian attitudes and behaviour, my inadequacies at home, my double standards as a preacher, my half-heartedness as a worshipper, my faltering steps as a disciple of the Lord Jesus. In response to the call to walk blamelessly, I limp along slowly. Before his watching eye I am frequently ashamed and I know I need help. But by God's mercy, through his Word and Spirit, I am finding the grace of forgiveness and the encouragement to keep moving forward.

One of the most pertinent and positive examples of integrity in Scripture comes from the life and ministry of the apostle Paul. His leadership model is countercultural, both in the first century and today. There was a wide range of situations in which Paul's character and leadership qualities were tested to the limit. Consequently, much of our supporting argument for Christian integrity will be taken from his second letter to the Corinthians. It is widely seen as one of the most personal and transparent letters that we have in Scripture. As we explore its themes, we get under his skin. His passions and frustrations are clear, as are his convictions and his leadership style. It is an extraordinary insight into the pressures and the joys of Christian service.

Whether responding to the criticisms showered upon him by the Corinthian congregation, or confronting the image-conscious super-apostles who had infiltrated the church, or administering finances in a transparent way, or struggling with personal weakness, pride and sustained opposition, Paul was acutely aware of God's call to 'walk before me and be blameless'. Time and again in his writing he underlines that his words, actions and attitudes are all seen by God and will be judged by him. He lives his life before God and he calls upon God as his witness. Paul helps us to see that integrity means leading with God watching.

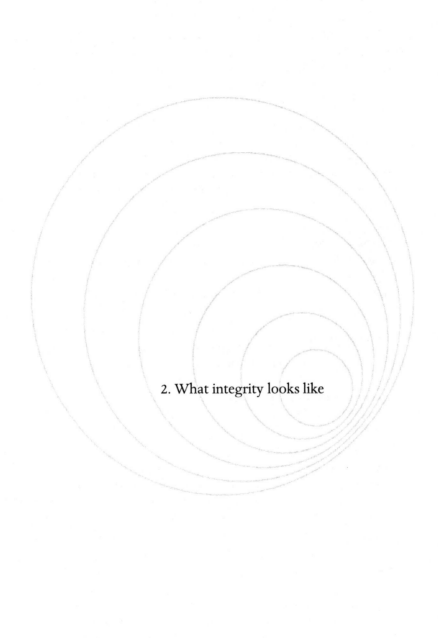

2. What integrity looks like

The former president of the Soviet Union, Mikhail Gorbachev, introduced his economic reforms under the banner of *perestroika*. In the book of that name, Gorbachev defined this as 'the unity of word and deeds'. He was concerned to ensure that political programmes were truly translated into economic reality, and that a population weary of decades of broken promises would be convinced by such a practical reform programme. He had a job on his hands.

For one thing, the populations of Communist countries at the time frequently mocked the inconsistencies so evident in their societies – and did so mostly through one of the few safe media, their jokes. In a recent article on Communist humour, Ben Lewis explained that such jokes were 'born of an absurd system which created a yawning gap between everyday experience and propaganda'. For example, here is a typical joke on the 'electronics gap' from the Democratic Republic of Germany: 'The latest achievements of the East German electronics company Robetron were celebrated – they built the world's largest micro-chip.'[1]

We have already seen that the same credibility gap exists in church life as in the worlds of politics and business. The need to live with integrity arises from the fact that we are called by a faithful God. His character is one of steadfast love and faithfulness, grace and truth, love and light. If we have come to know him, then we are called to express those same qualities, to walk in a way worthy of that calling, to live in conformity with his character. In this chapter we will see how Paul deliberately makes this connection.

Was Paul inconsistent?

The Corinthians were deeply suspicious of Paul's leadership qualities. In the next few chapters we will discover that he was criticized for a range of issues, but the letter begins with criticism that related to his apparent freedom to break promises and change plans. He was accused of being completely unreliable, promising to visit the Corinthians and then not turning up. He was accused of acting deviously and insincerely: instead of being transparent, he had been evasive.

At first sight it seems strange that the inspired Scriptures should give time to apparently mundane issues such as Paul's travel plans and letter-writing. But we will see that these issues, simple and ordinary though they may appear, reflect an attitude and a way of life which were critical not just in terms of Paul's leadership and credibility as an apostle, but also in relation to the message of the gospel which he proclaimed.

His relationship with the Corinthians helps us understand a great deal about the subject of leading with integrity. Leadership is essentially a relationship of trust. Credibility is fundamental.

Paul had worked with the Corinthians for some eighteen months, and as their pastor he had grown very close to them. He was proud of them, as a father is proud of his children. But things were going on in the church which were not worthy of the Christian community, and so Paul also had to issue a rebuke. He had to write to them in what appears to be rather severe terms. Anyone involved in church discipline will know that this is often an enormously costly exercise in terms of our emotional capital. The Corinthians certainly felt the pain. But for Paul, the exercise of discipline was very costly indeed, as we see from the tone of his expressions throughout this letter. The hope, of course, was that eventually the warmth and intimacy of their fellowship would be restored.

Unfortunately, it did not happen. There arrived in town a group of people who did all they could to undermine Paul's authority. They started a smear campaign, casting doubt on his credentials as a leader. This is a recurring theme throughout the letter and we will see how much of Paul's writing seeks to tackle the ungodly influence of these intruders. But the Corinthians were in no mood to accept Paul's rebuke and much preferred to accept the newly arrived critics. They succumbed to their persuasive rhetoric, and clearly began to have doubts about Paul's qualifications as an apostle and his integrity as a leader. In this atmosphere Paul was vulnerable to criticism from the Corinthians, and so when they learned of his decision to change his itinerary, that was the spark that ignited the gas.

What lay behind this? Paul had told the Corinthians that he would visit them twice on his next tour of Greece. But then he had to change his plans. It was a well-meaning decision, as we shall see, but it provided the Corinthians with the excuse for a barrage of hostile criticism, to which Paul now responds.

In chapter 1 we highlighted the fact that in all communities trust is of the essence. We will explore this more fully in chapter 7, but it was the first casualty in Paul's relationship with the Corinthians. Paul was a leader you could not trust, they said. He was deceitful. He made big promises but he failed to deliver. He was inconsistent and unreliable, making one decision today and changing his mind tomorrow. It is not hard to imagine the way in which such criticism gathered momentum, especially with the encouragement of the visitors in Corinth who were more than happy to provoke such betrayal.

Above and beyond such criticism, we will find throughout the letter an underlying accusation with which Paul must have found it particularly difficult to cope. It was the suggestion that he did not really care about them. Some of the Corinthians would have reasoned that the cumulative effect of a severe letter of rebuke and the broken promises of a cancelled visit meant that Paul had lost it. He could not be a true apostle who genuinely cared for his churches if he behaved like that. These verses are therefore particularly helpful in seeing what made Paul tick as a leader. They highlight three qualities which are essential to integrity.

Sincerity: pure motives

> Now this is our boast: Our conscience testifies that we have
> conducted ourselves in the world, and especially in our relations with
> you, in the holiness and sincerity that are from God. We have done
> so not according to worldly wisdom but according to God's grace.
> (2 Cor. 1:12)

The theme of boasting is prominent in 2 Corinthians, and it was something at which Paul's rivals were obviously skilled. Paul hated boasting about his achievements, as we see later in the letter, but this section highlights what he regarded to be of fundamental importance in his ministry. It is significant that he speaks so plainly of his integrity almost as a matter of personal pride.

Holiness and sincerity, he says, are the godly characteristics of his relationship with them. Some texts have the word 'simplicity' instead of 'holiness', because there are some manuscript variations, and this word seems most likely in the context. It stresses that Paul is straightforward, single-minded. It is the opposite of cunning or trickery. It is one of the attractive qualities of children interacting with their parents – spontaneous, unaffected directness. It is uncomplicated and out in the open. So, Paul says, that is how I deal with you too.

Sincerity implies that Paul's motives are unmixed and pure. We will look again at this word in due course, because Paul uses it in relation to his ministry. 'Unlike so many, we do not peddle the word of God for profit. On the contrary, in Christ we speak before God with sincerity, like men sent from God' (2:17). Everything is above board. He has acted in a direct and uncomplicated manner.

How has he been able to be so consistent? These qualities, he says in 1:12, come from God – and he has used them, the verse adds, 'according to God's grace'. So that is why he is able to boast with humility and not in a spirit of self-congratulation. He can take no credit. Only God can produce this integrity. This is one of many encouragements that we need to hear. Reading a book on integrity could induce a good deal of guilt or panic. We can feel it is all beyond us. Yet it is only by God's grace that we begin to reflect his character. He provides what we need to live as the gospel of grace demands.

These qualities – transparency, openness, directness, godly sincerity – are essential for leading with integrity. Too often leadership styles smell of manipulation, of political intrigue, of hidden agendas. It is precisely such attitudes which have led to public disillusionment with politics and big business and, sadly, with the church as an institution too. Paul was being criticized for exactly this kind of manipulative insincerity. You sense the atmosphere in his response later in his letter.

- 'We have renounced secret and shameful ways; we do not use deception.' (4:2)
- 'Make room for us in your hearts. We have wronged no one, we have corrupted no one, we have exploited no one.' (7:2)
- 'For such men are false apostles, deceitful workmen, masquerading as apostles of Christ. And no wonder, for Satan himself masquerades as an angel of light. It is not surprising, then, if his servants masquerade as servants of righteousness. Their end will be what their actions deserve.' (11:13–15)
- 'Did I exploit you through any of the men I sent you?' (12:17)

In contrast to the false apostles, whom Paul describes as masters of deception and insincerity, he was not guilty of unjust actions or of using his position to manipulate or exploit others. We do well to reflect on the tendencies in our own lives to abuse our positions of responsibility. It can happen in a variety of ways. For example:

- breaking confidences and talking about someone to a third party;
- misrepresenting others in our conversations or reports;
- creating mistrust;
- withholding information;
- using money as a lever.

Paul is adamant in chapter 1 in asserting that his conscience is clear; his motives, attitudes and behaviour are above board; he acts with frankness, transparency and godly sincerity. His reply then highlights a second personal quality.

Consistency: living life as a whole

First, he is consistent in all contexts. It is intriguing that he mentions that 'we have conducted ourselves in the world, and especially in our relations with you, in the holiness and sincerity that are from God' (1:12). His behaviour is the same in the world at large as it is in the church. He is not one person with unbelievers and another with Christians. I wonder if we could say the same of ourselves?

I once read an interesting news item which described the arrest of a German businessman: 'Heinrich K of Frankfurt has been given a 10 month suspended sentence and fined 1500 Marks for assaulting a traffic policeman. "Here's something for your mouth", shouted Heinrich, as he punched the policeman in the face after the policeman refused to remove the ticket from his illegally parked vehicle. Heinrich is an anger management consultant.'

Am I a different person at home from my image at work? Am I one person in my office, and another at church? Am I one person in a hotel room, or in the tax office, or in a traffic jam, and another in the pulpit? Paul stresses that he seeks to live in an entirely consistent manner: 'We have conducted ourselves in the world, and especially in our relations with you, in the holiness and sincerity that are from God' (1:12).

Second, he is consistent in his communication, whether written or spoken. As he says in the next verse, 'For we do not write to you anything you cannot read or understand. And I hope that, as you have understood us in part, you will come to understand fully . . . ' (1:13).

He presses the point by stating that, just as he is not guilty of double standards or inconsistency in his behaviour, so too he is not guilty of 'double talk' in his writing. He means what he says and he says what he means. There is no attempt to conceal or to deceive. He is not like the person who once wrote a reference for an employee applying for another job: struggling to know what to say, the employer wrote, 'If you knew him the way I know him, you would feel about him the same way I feel about him.'

His critics in Corinth made a big deal of this. We find it in chapter 10: 'For some say, "His letters are weighty and forceful, but in person he is unimpressive and his speaking amounts to nothing." Such people should realize that what we are in our letters when we are absent, we will be in our actions when we are present' (10:10–11). Paul's behaviour and his writing were unambiguous. He had no hidden agenda. There was no need to read between the lines, for his message was straightforward and reliable. It is a clear example of how the Christian life must be lived as a whole, with complete sincerity and consistency.

Third, he is consistent in his practical management. We find this later in the letter, as he describes the coordination of the relief fund, a theme which is dominant in 2 Corinthians 8 and 9. How Paul manages money is critical. It is a fundamental test of integrity and consistency, and we will devote some time to this in chapter 9. For now, let's notice how he is concerned to ensure that everything for which he is responsible is handled with the kind of consistency we have been examining. 'We want to avoid any criticism of the way we administer this liberal gift. For we are taking pains to do what is right, not only in the eyes of the Lord but also in the eyes of men' (8:20–21). He explains various practical ways in which he will ensure that this happens, to which we will turn later.

To demonstrate the seriousness with which he views this issue, he also underlines that he has acted consistently both before God and man. It is another statement of transparency. It is leading with God watching. He explicitly invokes God as the witness to the integrity of his motives and his decision-making. 'I call God as my witness that it was in order to spare you that I did not return to Corinth' (1:23). He repeats this in other sections of the letter, as we will see in the next chapter.

Paul has urged the Corinthians to accept his assurances with regard to his fundamental motivation – his utter sincerity and complete consistency. And all of this just because of a small change in the diary?

Paul, of course, realized what was at stake. It was not simply his credibility as an apostle. It was the credibility of the gospel message which he had brought to them. And that is why words like 'sincerity' and 'consistency' are so significant in our lives too. We know it matters. In a recent speech at Georgetown University in Washington, Tony Blair called on the West not to give up on its moral responsibilities to the subjugated peoples of the world. Yasmin Alibhai-Brown commented in *The Independent* that this was 'an idealistic message immediately contaminated by the messenger. His words sounded fraudulent, because he lied over Iraq and was contemptuous of the UN. What's more, he is a loser. His prototype mission in Iraq failed ... The resulting cynicism has since spread from east to west.'[2] Whatever our view of the intervention in Iraq and its aftermath, we understand her point: this was an idealistic message apparently contaminated by the messenger. People stop listening. They become cynical not just about the messenger, but also about the credibility of the message itself.

The reason for Paul's passionate response to the criticisms in Corinth arose from his concern to protect the truth, the apostolic message of the gospel. This was what really mattered. He responds in the same way in the closing paragraphs of his life, when he warns Timothy about Alexander the metalworker. Whoever he was, Alexander had done 'a great deal of harm' to Paul. In urging Timothy to be on his guard, however, what mattered for Paul was not the personal injury, but the fact that Alexander 'strongly opposed our message' (2 Tim. 4:14, 15). Whatever opposition Paul faced, the need to guard the gospel was always paramount.

Perhaps you are responsible for a church home group, and you tend to the conclusion that, in the scheme of things, this is relatively insignificant. It is just a matter of making sure there is somewhere to meet, someone to lead the discussion, someone to provide the coffee. But we should not lose sight of what Paul is saying. In the smallest of tasks, our responsibility is to ensure that there is a basic logic at work:

we are saying something about the truthfulness and power of the gospel when we serve faithfully and consistently. And we can be sure that, in the Christian community, we are being watched. How we handle the small and irritating jobs, how we respond to awkward customers in the group, how we communicate by email, how we respond when we are tired – in all of these ways we are saying something about our gospel values. This is the reason for Paul's passionate defence, and the reason for the call to live consistently.

Finally, there is a third personal quality which all leaders should emulate.

Reliability: reflecting God's faithfulness

In the last chapter we learned from the research of Margaret Thorsborne, who helps organizations manage workplace relationships and whose research placed integrity high on the list of essential qualities. Her writing is aimed at the secular market, and I was therefore intrigued to read her reference to a particular employee:

> Sarah is a middle manager in a large public sector organisation. She is one of the two people I can name who possess the virtue of integrity in spades. Sarah takes great care of people who are suffering. Utterly reliable, she is called on to fix things . . . Her commitment to management and staff wellbeing is enormous – often to her own personal cost, physically and emotionally. Her increasingly high profile and popularity amongst senior executive managers as reliable and trustworthy (she has saved their bacon on many an occasion) mean that she has been the subject of the 'tall poppy' syndrome. I suspect that by walking her talk, she has shamed other, less principled, colleagues in some way and so they have taken every opportunity to punish her. Snide comments, open hostility, formal complaints . . . a whisper in the ear of someone powerful – these all hurt her feelings badly. Despite this, she would not deviate from her work of transforming soured workplace relationships. She is a quietly committed Christian, and this obviously plays a significant role in her values.[3]

This is powerful stuff. Such a person is living a life that says a great deal about the coherence of the Christian faith. There is no question that it can be tough for anyone who lives like this, whether at work or in the

Christian community. Sincerity, consistency and reliability might be virtues most people admire, but on the ground it can get dirty. They are not attributes that are always welcomed.

Paul faced questions about his motives, and so once again defends his behaviour, this time with an emphasis on reliability. He now writes about his travel plans. He had hoped to visit them both on his way to Macedonia and on his way back, and he was not taking matters lightly as he prepared his itinerary. His motives were not selfish; in fact, his travel was planned entirely for their benefit, as he makes clear in 1:15. The word he uses here – translated 'benefit' – has an echo of the word for 'grace'. He wanted them to have a double blessing. When he was changing plans, he had their interests at heart.

He repeats the emphasis on reliability and sincerity by once again underlining his value system in verse 17. 'When I planned this, did I do it lightly? Or do I make my plans in a worldly manner so that in the same breath I say, "Yes, yes" and "No, no"?'

The Corinthians accused him of being completely unreliable: Paul? His words are 'Yes, yes, I'm coming to see you soon.' But what he really meant was 'No, no, I'm not coming back until much later.' You can't trust him . . . So Paul replies to such charges, 'But as surely as God is faithful, our message to you is not "Yes" and "No"' (v. 18).

He was not saying 'yes' and 'no' at the same time, or making promises one day only to break them the next. His plans were prepared thoughtfully in God's presence, for the good of the Corinthian believers. And verse 18 shows why this was so important for Paul: 'But as surely as God is faithful, our message to you is not "Yes" and "No".'

As we have seen, he was not just defending his personal reputation. Any criticism of his trustworthiness would cast doubt over the trustworthiness of his ministry and therefore of his message. His response is to speak first of God's faithfulness, and then of his own trustworthiness.

God's faithfulness and ours

> But as surely as God is faithful, our message to you is not 'Yes' and
> 'No'. For the Son of God, Jesus Christ, who was preached among you
> by me and Silas and Timothy, was not 'Yes' and 'No', but in him it has

always been 'Yes'. For no matter how many promises God has made, they are 'Yes' in Christ. And so through him the 'Amen' is spoken by us to the glory of God. Now it is God who makes both us and you stand firm in Christ. He anointed us, set his seal of ownership on us, and put his Spirit in our hearts as a deposit, guaranteeing what is to come. (1:18–21)

There are three evidences of the reality of God's faithfulness, Paul says.

- First, Jesus Christ, God's Son, is God's 'Yes'. In Jesus there is no inconsistency. He is the model of integrity, the embodiment of God's faithfulness (1:19).
- Second, God has fulfilled – and continues to fulfil – every one of his promises through his Son, Jesus Christ. And like the Corinthians, we too affirm God's faithfulness when through Christ we say 'Amen' to the preaching of God's Word (1:20).
- Third, God has given his Spirit to us – to Paul, to the Corinthians, to all of God's people (1:21).

Why does Paul take time to outline a doctrinal theme in the midst of a practical defence? All the metaphors of verse 21 show that the Spirit had equipped Paul not only to be a vehicle for God's promises, but also to be a living demonstration of their trustworthiness. To doubt Paul's reliability would be to doubt the credibility of the work of the Spirit in his and their lives. To doubt Paul's word would be to doubt the credibility of the gospel Word. How can he, God's messenger, act in a way which is inconsistent with the God who sends him?

It is a remarkably bold affirmation of his integrity. He is so concerned about the accusations being made against him that he dares to draw a parallel between his action and God's. As surely as God is faithful, he stresses, so is our word. Just as God keeps his promises, so do we. Paul's response to the charges against him was not only to repudiate them vigorously but, in so doing, to demonstrate how reliable the Christian message is. And what about the proof? It is:

- founded on God's faithfulness;
- secured through Christ's work;
- guaranteed by the Spirit's presence in our lives.

Let me ask, then, to what extent are these personal qualities evident in our leadership? Sincerity, consistency and reliability: failure to demonstrate integrity in these ways is quite possibly the most serious obstacle in any form of Christian ministry and, indeed, in the growth of God's work. Is it possible that outsiders look at our organization or church or leadership and see nothing distinctively Christian about the way we use people, or handle money, or fulfil our mission statements, or keep our promises?

We have seen from Paul's testimony that we are especially in need of God's grace if we are to live like this. In our Christian communities we should pray more often than we do that we will know a fresh empowering of the Spirit, equipping us in the holiness and sincerity that are from God. For, if that happens, it will not only transform us and our Christian fellowship, but will provide an authentic model of how the gospel works. It will honour the name of Christ, the one who truly demonstrates God's integrity and reliability.

Section A – Over to you . . .

- God says, 'Walk before me and be blameless.' To what extent do you live your life in the conscious awareness of God's presence? In what areas do you know there is inconsistency in your life, which you long to address through the power of God's Word and Spirit? What are the key areas of growth you would like to see in your personal walk?
- Can people rely completely on your word? Do you follow through in your commitments and honour your promises?
- We all face the temptation to adjust our presentation of a situation according to our audience. Is your speech always truthful, irrespective of the person to whom you are speaking?
- We have different personalities, with some more committed to the big picture and others to the details. But to what extent are you reliable in completing the task you have been given, ensuring your responsibilities are carried out faithfully?
- Are you the same person in a traffic jam, a hotel room, a tax office and a family argument as you are in the church or the pulpit?

B. Leadership and calling

3. True accountability

> Imagine, as we all sometimes do, your entire life as a surveillance film, shot neutrally and unjudgementally as if by a CCTV camera. Then imagine it being shown to the world – partners, friends, work colleagues. You are shown stripped bare, your mendacities and play-acting revealed for all to see. In the old stories, God used to play this role. These days the all-seeing being is the digital camera, which in the real world does indeed play judge and jury for countless little crimes, and some big ones.

Rosie Millard wrote these lines in a review of the film *Caché* ('Hidden'). It is essentially a simple morality tale: does personal integrity depend on who is watching? And Millard concludes, 'These days, it's best to be squeaky clean right deep down inside. Big Brother is watching all of us.'[1]

Most of us indulge in a degree of play-acting for the cameras, of course. When in public our manners improve, our dress might be smarter, our annoying habits under control, even our accent slightly more proper. But that is not the real issue. The question is multi-layered: does our public life match our private behaviour, and does our private behaviour match our inner life? As a child I can still recall evangelists at our small London church asking us how we would feel if our life was played out on a big movie screen in the church hall. That did not worry me too much. I was a pretty ordinary thirteen-year-old with a rather pedestrian daily life. But what would have induced a degree of panic would have been a screening of my inner life, my reactions to my siblings, my thoughts about my teachers, my less than Christian attitudes to people in the congregation.

Living with integrity is not motivated in the first instance from the fear that private behaviour or innermost thoughts might some day be disclosed for the world to see, although that certainly would concentrate the mind. Instead, the greatest motivation to live a life of integrity arises from a sense of gratitude. I want to live this way because it is an expression of my accountability to the God who loves me and who has called me to serve him.

I have become more aware as I grow older of the powerful and positive influence of a sense of accountability. I am accountable to many people. I am responsible to my family, aware of promises made to my wife to live faithfully, 'forsaking all others'. I am acutely aware of my responsibility to my three daughters, for whom I must care with serious attention and loving commitment. These four women in my life have every right to flag up my inconsistency – they watch my life and know my weaknesses.

I am responsible as an employee to fulfil my obligations to my employer. And as an employee of a Christian organization, I am accountable to some degree to individuals and churches whose generosity funds our work and provides our salaries. I do not labour with a sense of guilt, but with a sense of gratitude. Nevertheless, the fact that people have given sacrificially calls me to exercise a careful stewardship. Then I am responsible to my colleagues around the world, playing my part in operations that support the cause of our mission. Come to that, I am responsible to the Inland Revenue, since as a British citizen I must ensure that I declare my income and pay my dues, not least because ultimately it is for the well-being of the society of which I am a part.

I feel accountable that, having received such good gifts, I should live with responsible stewardship and true gratitude. I know that I must live before my children in a way that sets an example they would wish to follow, and that I must live with my wife, friends and colleagues in a way that is consistent with the claims I make from pulpits and conference platforms.

But we all know there are ways to dodge or soften these responsibilities. I read recently that Japanese businessmen could purchase 'alibi tapes'. If they wish to stay behind at the office for a secret liaison with a woman, they can telephone their wife and play the small cassette at the same time. It provides background sounds of a railway station or busy airport, so that the man can suggest his train is cancelled or his flight delayed. Most of us use more subtle techniques. We can excuse, deceive, tell half-truths, cut corners.

The call to integrity comes with greatest force as I understand my accountability to God himself. I need to be careful here, for it would be a mistake to suggest that I serve God with fear, that I imagine him to be the great employer, the ultimate taxman. No, my accountability to God arises from my status as someone made in his image, called to be his child, and as a person redeemed by his grace to serve him freely and wholeheartedly.

True, I am also accountable – as are all men and women – as a person created by him and morally responsible to him. But my sense of accountability and therefore my Christian service is especially shaped by my response to his gracious call. This makes a huge difference to me. When I am tempted to become casual in my work or attitudes, or to behave in ways which do not commend Christ, I am cheapening the grace of God.

Although Paul is writing to defend his actions to the Corinthians, he is especially concerned to underline that his primary accountability is to God. Time and again he repeats the assertion that he lives his life under God's watching eye, the theme which has given this book its subtitle.

It is worth pausing to see how frequently Paul mentions this. Below is a cluster of references to make the point.

God sees
'God as my witness' (1:23)
'in the sight of Christ' (2:10)
'in the sight of God' (4:2)
'in the eyes of the Lord [and] men' (8:21)
'in the sight of God' (12:19)

God knows
'What we are is plain to God' (5:11)
'God knows I do' (11:11)
'God ... knows that I am not lying' (11:31)
'God knows' (12:2, 3)

God cares
'In the day of the Lord Jesus' (1:14)
'we speak before God with sincerity' (2:17)
'before God' (3:4)
'before the judgment seat of Christ' (5:10)
'out of reverence for God' (7:1)
'before God' (7:12)
'honour the Lord' (8:19)
'one whom the Lord commends' (10:18)

He knows that he is accountable to God. In chapter 1 we noted that a feature of Paul's consistency was that he could call God as his witness as he defended his action (1:23), and throughout his letter he underlines that all of his actions and attitudes are known by God himself: 'What we are is plain to God, and I hope it is also plain to your conscience' (5:11); 'We have been speaking in the sight of God' (12:19).

I find Paul's emphasis very challenging. There is nothing casual about his ministry. The way he fulfils his responsibility to proclaim Christ, the way in which he behaves under criticism, the manner of his decision-making – everything is done under God's watching eye. There is not a hint of indifference in his Christian service.

So although he is reluctant to commend himself, as we shall see, he is able to respond with complete honesty because he knows he stands before God and is accountable to him. Because of the frequency with which Paul expresses this commitment to accountability and transparency, with his use of the phrase 'before God', some commentators suggest it might even be a kind of oath formula. He is deadly serious.

Paul realizes that his motives, his attitudes and his behaviour matter to God. He 'speaks before God' (2:17). He acts 'out of reverence for God' (7:1). He knows that everything will one day come under God's scrutiny – 'in the day of the Lord Jesus' (1:14). It is very clear in chapter 5 as he describes his motivation for service: 'We make it our goal to please him . . . ' (5:9). And he continues, 'For we must all appear before the judgment seat of Christ, that each one may receive what is due to him for the things done while in the body, whether good or bad' (5:10). So one day I will stand before Jesus Christ, who sent me as an ambassador, and I will give an account of what I have done. Paul does not take this lightly. 'Since, then, we know what it is to fear the Lord . . . ' (5:11).

The judgment which Paul describes is not a judgment concerning our eternal destiny. Rather, it will be a time for giving an account of how we have lived our lives, a judgment on our stewardship. This verse is best understood when placed alongside Paul's teaching in his first letter to the Corinthians (1 Cor. 3:11–15). He writes there of the importance of ensuring that our lives are built on the foundation of Christ. He is the one foundation, who will withstand all tests. We are secure if our lives are built on him. But there is more to be said. The question remains, how will we build on that foundation? Will we build with those things which are short-lived – wood, hay, straw – or will we build with those things which are of lasting value – gold, silver, precious stones? One day the quality of our building work will be tested, and on that judgment day will it survive or will it disappear in a cloud of smoke? The point is clear: how you build matters; how you live your life counts. Paul refers to the fact that the judgment we will face on that day will be a very practical one – 'for the things done while in the body, whether good or bad' (5:10).

Everything will be out in the open. That judgment day for Christians is not intended to cloud our hope or dampen our joy at the prospect of being with Christ. Rather, it is there as a stimulus to faithful service, a reminder of our obligations to live for Christ, to live our lives under his control and direction. How do I use my time, my gifts, my resources and the many God-given opportunities? All these things matter, Paul says, in the light of the future. Will we look back on our lives and see that we have built only things that are temporary, or will we have built something that will last, something for eternity? So it is a stimulus to faithful service, a call to be wholehearted in living for the values of God's kingdom, not building for personal and therefore for temporary gain.

In an interview on Michael Parkinson's talk show, Tony Blair made a rare confession with regard to how his faith impacted his political decisions. He suggested that God would have a role in judging his actions concerning the war in Iraq. *The Times* reported on the reaction to his comments: 'The intolerance of secular Britain was shown by those who seem to regard any belief as a sign of weakness . . . Britain is ill-served by the resulting hysterical and militant secularism.' Certainly he was mocked for adopting this position. Here is Richard Reeves in the *New Statesman*: 'It really doesn't matter if he prayed with George W. Bush: if it happened, it was in private and they are both consenting adults. It does matter if Blair believes, as he appears to, that his ultimate responsibility for sending us to war is to his Maker. Blair's responsibility is on earth to the families of those injured or killed.'[2]

Tony Blair explained that he was accountable both to the British electorate and also to God, before whom he would stand in judgment for his actions and decisions. In this regard, he was absolutely right, and it would make a considerable difference to political style, behaviour and decision-making if all politicians were to have this same conviction.

In one of the most moving of his letters, written in the closing months of his life, Paul urged Timothy to live with this same sense of accountability. 'In the presence of God and of Christ Jesus, who will judge the living and dead, and in view of his appearing and his kingdom, I give you this charge . . .' (2 Tim. 4:1). Paul looked back over years of service and could with good conscience declare that he had lived with a true sense of accountability and responsibility towards God, the Judge whom he was shortly to meet.

> I have fought the good fight, I have finished the race, I have kept the
> faith. Now there is in store for me the crown of righteousness, which
> the Lord, the righteous Judge, will award to me on that day – and
> not only to me, but also to all who have longed for his appearing.
> (2 Tim. 4:7–8)

While this injects a seriousness to our ministry, there is also a sense of liberation, especially when we are facing criticism. As Paul says in his earlier Corinthian letter, 'I care very little if I am judged by you . . . It is the Lord who judges me' (1 Cor. 4:3, 4). He says much the same in his first letter to the Thessalonians. His motives are clear; he is not trying to trick them. 'On the contrary, we speak as men approved by God to be entrusted with the gospel. We are not trying to please men but God, who tests our hearts' (1 Thess. 2:3–4). In a similar way to Paul's writing in 2 Corinthians, he is replying to his critics who claimed he was not a true apostle. So he explains in direct terms that his ministry was based on being commissioned by God. God had approved him and sent him. Now he felt a deep sense of responsibility, because he had been entrusted with the gospel. He was a steward with a deep sense of trusteeship and this gripped him, transforming his life and shaping his priorities.

In turn, his calling shaped his motives and behaviour. 'We are not trying to please men but God, who tests our hearts. You know we never used flattery, nor did we put on a mask to cover up greed – God is our witness. We were not looking for praise from men, not from you or anyone else' (1 Thess. 2:4–5). You get the feel for the accusations he faced from his choice of words: 'error . . . impure motives . . . trick . . . flattery . . . cover up . . . greed' (1 Thess. 2:3, 5, 6). How do you respond to criticism? It is one of the toughest tests of our

Christian calling and can sometimes place our commitment to integrity under severe strain. It bruises our ego, drains our motivation, takes the spring from our step and can push us towards resentment, anger and frustration. Why am I doing all this when it is thrown back in my face?

One great advantage of criticism is that it forces you to test your fundamental motivations. For Paul it was clear: 'We are not trying to please men but God ... We were not looking for praise from men' (1 Thess. 2:4, 6). There were no mixed motives. He was transparently honest. There was no deceit, no cover-up, no greed. Everything was above board. He was quite upfront about it: 'You know ... God is our witness ... You are witnesses, and so is God' (1 Thess. 2: 5, 10).

We cannot miss the point. Integrity means living with God watching, for God is concerned with every part of our life, even those parts which are unseen to others. Some challenging questions follow.

- Who are we when no one is looking?
- How do we work when the boss is away?
- Do we sustain our working hours and focused priorities when we work from home?
- If no one is watching, are we good at time-keeping, scrupulous in our use of money, careful about the websites we visit?

Our work will be transformed as we understand that we are responsible to our Father and accountable to our Judge – and this helps in our service of others. In writing for church leaders, Peter Brain says, 'If we assume we are the church's servants, we will find ourselves with a master we cannot possibly please. How can we serve a master with many and varied voices? ... Clearly we serve God and belong to him, and have been called and commissioned by him to be his servants. We will serve the church best by serving him.'[3]

We should not imagine, however, that our accountability is to God alone. One of the ways in which this is likely to be expressed is in our relationships with fellow Christians. For many Christian leaders, the lack of any sensible human accountability is a major weakness in their lives. We desperately need others to hold us accountable. We will say more about the team context of our work shortly, but one great advantage of working alongside others is that we benefit from both support and accountability. For some reason, Christians are rather reluctant to discuss performance reviews, measurement and accountability. But whether we approach this formally or informally, a sense of our responsibility for others and our accountability to others is an essential element of ensuring we live with integrity.

Paul worked in team contexts, and encouraged others to do so. On his first missionary journey he was sent out by a team, worked with a team and reported back to the team. This is neatly expressed at the close of his journey with Luke's summary statement in Acts 14:26–28: '... they sailed back to Antioch, where they had been committed to the grace of God for the work they had now completed. On arriving there, they gathered the church together and reported all that God had done through them and how he had opened the door of faith to the Gentiles. And they stayed there a long time with the disciples.' There are three expressions of accountability here.

Accountability to God: 'all that God had done through [or with] them' (Acts 14:27). It is an acknowledgment that God had done the work. Their ministry was the result of his calling, his care, his empowering; it was carried out under his watchful eye. Accountability to God will mean a growing sense of dependence on him, a deliberate refocusing on our calling and a commitment to ensure that we are fulfilling our work and service for his glory and good purposes.

Accountability to others: 'they gathered the church together and reported' (Acts 14:27). That was clearly a wonderful way to thank, but also to encourage, their fellow believers back in Antioch. And it is also a significant ingredient of integrity, since we must be accountable to others. There are various ways in which we can do this. In formal terms, we might be responsible to an employer, a parochial church council or a board. These structures are important for support and strategic guidance, but we need to make sure that accountability works. Leaders need accountability to keep focused on their task, and without this we can easily misuse our power, even in Christian settings. We can manipulate situations for our own benefit. The problem is that accountability to others is often very limited. Leaders can carefully control the situation, because the formal group (the PCC, the board) only knows what the leader tells them; so we must find ways of ensuring that there is true accountability which encourages transparency and honesty.

There are also many non-formal ways of remaining accountable to others, and usually these have to be quite intentional. It might be through a small prayer triplet, where we meet with two other close friends, praying for our shared concerns and being open with each other about our struggles and temptations as well as our hopes and our joys. In a church setting the ideal is a context of shared leadership, which has within it the support, trust and accountability which we need. This makes demands upon us: we need to set aside time to talk and pray together; we need to be willing to be honest about our successes and failures, trusting our fellow believers to handle the information with integrity; and we need to be ready to share the burdens of fellow leaders too. But it is an essential foundation for living consistently. Without such accountability to others, we can easily deceive ourselves. We can live two lives, one governed by our internal script, a secret life that is unknown to others, and a public life, which might appear crisp and clean but is not the true person.

Accountability for ourselves: 'the work they had now completed' (Acts 14:26). As Paul and Barnabas reported back, they were very aware that God had carried out his work through them. The passage underlines repeatedly that it was the Spirit who was at work. Yet remarkably, after a tour of several cities and the planting and nurturing of young Christian communities, they sensed a job well done. The work to which God had called them had been completed. There is also a sense, then, in which we are accountable for our own lives and for fulfilling the work with which we have been entrusted. We certainly do so with God watching and with God empowering. But we are accountable for our own management of time, our responsible service, our deeper understanding of Scripture and our growth in leadership. This should not be self-centred, but should be shaped by our determination to mature as a servant leader, more able to fulfil the Lord's calling.

In all of these ways we are following the Master, who was committed to his Father's will. Throughout the Gospels we see that single-minded obedience to the Father was the driving force of Jesus' life. He was sent by him, empowered by him, in fellowship with him and obedient to him. Our discipleship must be the same. As Paul expressed it to the Corinthians, 'we make it our goal to please him' (2 Cor. 5:9). That is the heart of living with integrity.

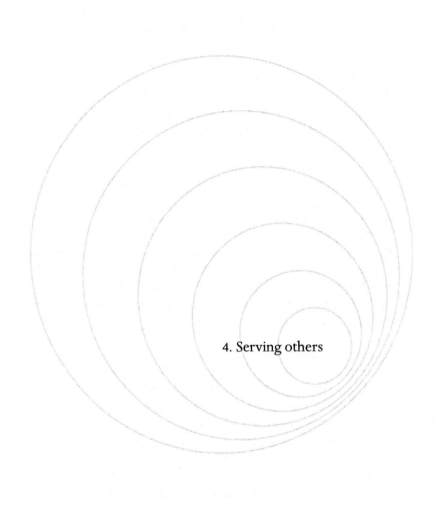

4. Serving others

I have recently received news of two bishops. One of my colleagues returned from an African country where we have been working with nationals to develop a training programme for pastors. Some 160 men and women were involved, but one leader stood out. He was the bishop. But he was not on the stage giving the lectures. My friend described how the bishop was the one quietly going round the room collecting the used water bottles. When someone came into the crowded hall and could not find a chair, the bishop was the one who made it his job to ensure a chair was found. The second bishop is a senior Anglican in the UK. He is a controversial figure, frequently in the news media, and a master of the sound bite. Fair enough, we might suppose. Yet it seems to some of the Christians in his city that 'he's never happy unless he's in the headlines'.

The comments made to me about both bishops are, of course, simple snapshots. We cannot judge motives, and the bishops serve in very different cultures. But they do at least raise a question about how we view our service. What is its primary orientation? In describing Timberline Church, Colorado, Jeff Lucas quotes a simple principle about leadership expressed by his senior pastor. He suggests that when most leaders walk into the room, their attitude is 'here I am' – and they work hard to impress, to be noticed. But the pastor encourages his fellow leaders to throw away 'here I am' and replace it with 'there you are'. It is simple but very perceptive. It says a good deal about the primary orientation of our leadership.

The literature on leadership increasingly uses the language of service. For the past thirty years, the description 'servant leader' has been applied to the business world almost as much as within the church. A moment's thought shows us that this ought to be obvious. After all, leadership can only be defined in relation to other people, and the most effective leadership seeks purposefully to influence, equip and therefore to serve others. It may be obvious, but its fulfilment could not be more demanding. Serving others is fraught with challenges, as we shall see in the chapters which follow. It is not simply to do with the demands made by those whom we seek to serve. Perhaps more demanding still, we have our own personal agenda to contend with. Serving others does not come naturally to us. We are often motivated in our work by self-interest, reflected in our concerns for self-preservation and self-promotion which often lie just below the surface. Too often we who wish to be servant leaders are little more than self-serving.

The orientation of Christian service: 'for your sake'

For our leadership to have integrity, it is essential not only to have a clear understanding of our calling to serve God, to whom we are accountable, but also to see that this necessarily means a calling to serve others. You know servant leaders when you see them: people whose first concern is your best interests; people who carry out their work for the well-being of the community or organization they serve; people who go to almost any length to care for us.

Acting in such a way is all the more challenging when your service is thrown back in your face. 'Well, if that's what they think, I'll leave them to it. I'll go where my ministry is appreciated!' Paul's servant leadership was certainly put to the test by his fellow believers in Corinth. As we saw in 2 Corinthians 1, he was greeted with suspicion and accused of insincerity. Despite having brought them the gospel, and despite his many overtures of love and concern, here was a community who doubted his motives, criticized his best efforts and rejected his service.

Serving others, even those who reject us, is part of our Christian calling. We are doing nothing other than following the service of the Master. Jesus made the connection between service and rejection when he spoke to his disciples. 'For even the Son of Man did not come to be served, but to serve, and to give his life as a ransom for many' (Mark 10:45). Yet somehow we have lost the perspective of service. As Kent and Barbara Hughes comment, 'There is a mindset ... that defines success as a kind of lordship: sitting in the honoured seat, being the fêted guest at luncheons, speaking to vast throngs, building monuments, collecting honorary titles. Whatever you call it, it's a philosophy that values the business of being served.'[1] It is not a new phenomenon: Jude described it in his epistle. He calls the false teachers 'shepherds who feed only themselves', an echo of Ezekiel's condemnation of the leaders in Israel who cared for themselves rather than for the Lord's flock.[2]

So is my attitude 'here I am' or 'there you are'? It will not be easy, but it is worth pausing regularly to evaluate your motives. You are holding a responsibility in the church which takes a great deal of time and energy; you give up other things which you would have liked to do in order to take on the role; and you are faced with criticism. I am afraid it happens. It is not always intentionally hurtful, but when you have given of your best, and you are tired and drained, the critical reactions of others can be very wounding. That is the best time to assess if you are truly following in your Master's footsteps.

There is a simple phrase to remember in this situation, and once again it is borrowed from Paul. We have seen how he lived his life under the watchful eye of God himself, serving him faithfully as a good steward. But he also said on several occasions that his actions were motivated by a concern for the well-being of his fellow Christians. Here is the test: 'for your sake'. I am doing this for you. I am fulfilling my responsibility to God by fulfilling my responsibility to you. You find the two together in Paul's tender writing in 2 Corinthians 4. 'We who are alive are always being given over to death *for Jesus' sake* ... All this is *for your benefit*' (4:11, 15, my italics). Earlier in the chapter he has said that we are 'your servants for Jesus' sake' (4:5). And, as we will see when we come to confronting failure, Paul said, 'I have forgiven in the sight of Christ *for your sake*' (2:10, my italics). So he is implying that all he went through in the ups and downs of his ministry experience was for their sake because it was for Jesus' sake. At the end of the letter the emphasis is the same: 'we are weak in him, yet by God's power we will live with him to serve you' (13:4). It is for their benefit.

I wonder: for the sake of others? That is a test of servant leadership.

What are the elements that characterize service with integrity? Paul makes it clear.

> So I made up my mind that I would not make another painful visit to you. For if I grieve you, who is left to make me glad but you whom I have grieved? I wrote as I did so that when I came I should not be distressed by those who ought to make me rejoice. I had confidence in all of you, that you would all share my joy. For I wrote to you out of great distress and anguish of heart and with many tears, not to grieve you but to let you know the depth of my love for you.
> (2 Cor. 2:1–4)

It is possible that the disciplinary action to which Paul refers in chapter 2 is the same issue about which he wrote in 1 Corinthians – someone who was guilty of sexual immorality. But I tend to agree with recent commentators that this chapter might have more to do with an injury that Paul himself sustained at the hands of the Corinthian church. We will talk more about this in chapter 8. What is clear in Paul's writing is his deeply felt emotion.

Vulnerability in Christian service
As Paul wrote his letter his heart was broken, his eyes filled with tears. The reason for cancelling his proposed visit was that he could not face the emotional trauma. Many of us know that experience: the feeling in the pit of the stomach as we anticipate what we have to confront. And in the text one word group is very prominent. It does not take too much imagination to get the picture:

- 'painful' (2:1);
- 'grieve' (2:2);
- 'distressed' (2:3);
- 'great distress and anguish of heart' (2:4).

There is no doubt that Paul felt acute anxiety in his pastoral work with the church. There was no cool professionalism. He felt the pain and was not afraid to admit it. There are other references in the letter too:

- 'I still had no peace of mind' (2:13);
- 'conflicts on the outside, fears within' (7:5);
- 'Besides everything else, I face daily the pressure of my concern for all the churches' (11:28).

This kind of pain is unavoidable in Christian ministry. Engagement with others, particularly in pastoral support, brings its inevitable sorrows. Paul lived with a transparency and vulnerability that we would do well to emulate. Listen to how he writes to Timothy: 'You, however, know all about my teaching, my way of life, my purpose, faith, patience, love, endurance, persecutions, sufferings . . .' (2 Tim. 3:10–11). Whether it was with his close friends, the churches for which he cared, or even his opponents, Paul was unafraid to expose his emotions. He refused to keep a professional distance. 'You know all about me.' 'I wrote to you out of great distress and anguish of heart and with many tears.'

Vulnerability is costly, of course, but detachment is not an option in leadership that is modelled on Christ's service. It is almost impossible to remain neutral if we are human, and if we are giving our lives to serve others. There is a necessary commitment to our own personal care, of course, since the kind of vulnerability we are describing does take its toll. 'Burnout' is the result of a range of factors, but one of the most significant relates to the pain and distress we must sometimes carry. But the path of wisdom lies not in avoiding the costs of ministry, but in ensuring there are mechanisms in place to share the load and discover the resources which can compensate for such pain and help preserve emotional balance.

Leading with integrity will inevitably mean this kind of vulnerability. We cannot protect ourselves from such demands in Christian ministry. We can only seek the comfort of the Spirit and the encouragement of our fellow workers.

Sacrificial love

> For I wrote you out of great distress and anguish of heart and with many tears, not to grieve you but to let you know the depth of my love for you. (2 Cor. 2:4)

The word 'love' here is emphatic, and it is an impressive feature of Paul's integrity. Later in the letter he tells them, 'I will very gladly spend for you everything I have and expend myself as well' (12:15). He said the same to the Thessalonians: 'We loved you so much that we were delighted to share with you not only the gospel of God but our lives as well, because you had become so dear to us' (1 Thess. 2:8).

How do you respond to people who have injured you in some way? Or to people who have acted unjustly, or have spoken against you or sought to harm your reputation? Or to people who have cynically rejected your attempts to help? This was exactly Paul's situation. Yet by God's grace he is able to affirm a depth of love for those very people. How does this work? As we saw in the last chapter, our calling makes the difference. Our primary accountability is towards God himself. And as we see this as a fundamental priority, it will in turn shape our concern for others.

In his moving address to the Ephesian leaders, Paul points to the link between our sense of accountability to God and our sense of service towards his people. 'Keep watch over yourselves and all the flock of which the Holy Spirit has made you overseers. Be shepherds of the church of God, which he bought with his own blood' (Acts 20:28).

John Stott points to the trinitarian ring of this verse as he highlights the profound privilege of giving ourselves wholeheartedly to the care of others – to shepherd the flock for which God himself gave his Son.

> This splendid Trinitarian affirmation, that the pastoral oversight of the church belongs to God (Father, Son and Holy Spirit), should have a profound effect on pastors. It should humble us to remember that the church is not ours, but God's. And it should inspire us to faithfulness . . . They are the flock of God the Father, purchased by the precious blood of God the Son, and supervised by overseers appointed by God the Holy Spirit. If the three persons of the Trinity are thus committed to the welfare of the people, should we not be also?[3]

Paul must have had this beating deep in his heart as he responded to the Corinthian criticisms. And such a perspective helps us greatly in those situations where leading others can be particularly demanding. It is not that I must manufacture affection for those for whom I have responsibility. It is rather a love born of the Spirit, a compassion that naturally arises when we serve God, sense his priorities and long for the well-being of those for whom Christ gave his life. In writing about the subject of preaching, Colin Morris also describes how sacrificial engagement with others is an essential companion to the spoken word: 'It is not from a pulpit but a cross that power-filled words are spoken. Sermons need to be seen as well as heard to be effectual. Eloquence, homiletical skills, biblical knowledge are not enough. Anguish, pain, engagement, sweat and blood punctuate the stated truths to which men will listen.'[4]

Parental concern
We discover throughout the letter that Paul was willing to offer his life for the sake of his dear children. Part of the slanderous accusations

made against him appear to have arisen from the fact that he charged no fee for his services. He was an amateur, they said, a con man. Paul replies to this charge, in effect, 'I see myself as your spiritual father. Would a father demand payment for his parental services from his children?' (see 2 Cor. 12:14–15).

Admittedly, children sometimes demand payment for doing housework or their school homework. But Paul makes the point in a very moving statement: 'Children should not have to save up for their parents, but parents for their children. So I will very gladly spend for you everything I have and expend myself as well' (12:15). This was the reason why Paul appealed for an open relationship with them. 'As a fair exchange – I speak as to my children – open wide your hearts also' (6:13). He uses the idea of parenting in other passages, even suggesting to the Galatians that he was suffering from labour pains until Christ was formed in them (Gal. 4:19). But perhaps most obviously, he uses the language of parenthood in the passage in 1 Thessalonians to which we have already referred. 'We were gentle among you, like a mother caring for her little children . . . For you know that we dealt with each of you as a father deals with his own children, encouraging, comforting and urging you to live lives worthy of God, who calls you into his kingdom and glory' (1 Thess. 2:7, 11–12).

While not having children of his own in a human family, Paul expressed extraordinary parental love and concern for those who had come to faith through his ministry. There is tenderness in his appeals to the Corinthians: 'I speak as to my children – open wide your hearts' (2 Cor. 6:13). He felt both the joys and the sorrows of caring for them. He experienced the grief of being rejected by them; he felt the pain of disciplining them; he knew the joy of seeing them restored.

The imagery of parental love is a helpful one when it comes to assessing the integrity of our service. I am very aware of my weaknesses as a father, but my wife Margaret and I share a longing for the very best for our children. I think we can say that we will gladly lay aside all other things for their well-being. We do not see our care for them, which now spans some twenty-two years, as in any sense a sacrifice. We can understand Paul's language as he expresses his willingness to spend his life for them. And Christian service must express exactly these same qualities. We must be careful with the suggestion of 'parenting', for we are fellow believers, equally dependent on the Father himself. But the language of parental concern conjures up the right images – not self-seeking or self-serving, but self-giving. It is once again expressed by Paul as 'for your sake'. As he says in the same section, 'We have been speaking in the sight of God as those in Christ; and everything we do, dear friends, is for your strengthening' (12:19).

His approach to fellow believers, then, is shot through with integrity. Indeed, we can say that his leadership is a reflection of Jesus himself. It is modelled on his sacrificial love, his vulnerable service. Perhaps the most obvious statement of Paul's leadership style is found in 10:1: 'By the meekness and gentleness of Christ, I appeal to you . . .' These are the qualities that characterize Christ's dealings with us, and this was the model for Paul's leadership and ministry. These same qualities of gentleness and forbearance are listed by Paul in the pastoral epistles as essential for those exercising authority. They are qualities that do not usually appear in the top-down hierarchical models of leadership that sometimes influence our thinking and behaviour, but they are qualities which respect the weak and care for the vulnerable.

Let us summarize. We have seen from 2 Corinthians 1 and 2 that Paul's defence is given when he is under very significant pressure. Yet even so, he is able to speak confidently – before God himself and in the light of his ultimate judgment – of his absolute commitment to integrity. He wished to speak and act with sincerity, consistency and reliability. He wished to display these qualities in all contexts, public and private, in secular or Christian environments. And he wished his relationships with the Corinthians – who were presently causing him such pain and injury – to be marked by genuine affection. He was ready for the costs of that service, including potential rejection; he was open-hearted, not defensive; and he cared for others as a father for his dearly loved children.

This is the kind of authentic leadership that matters. It may not get us into the headlines; it may mean going unnoticed, picking up the water bottles and helping with the chairs. But we will be showing the integrity of Christ himself, who picked up the towel and washbasin. Serving God with integrity means 'there you are', not 'here I am'. Its orientation is always 'for your sake'.

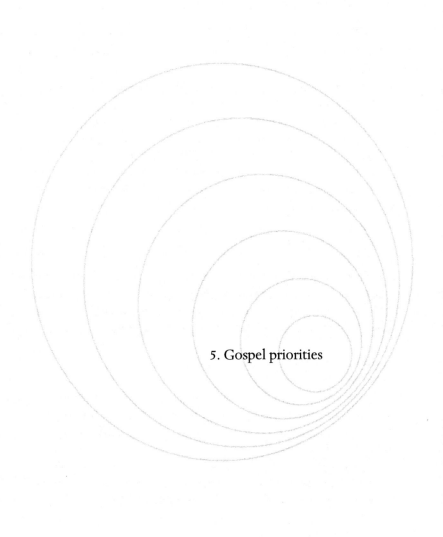

5. Gospel priorities

I was recently sent the results of an interesting survey which listed all the qualities that people expect from the perfect pastor. This is what the computerized survey indicated.

- The perfect pastor preaches for exactly twelve minutes.
- He is twenty-eight years of age, but he has been preaching for thirty years.
- He works from 8.00 a.m. until midnight every day, but is also the caretaker.
- He frequently condemns sin, but never upsets anyone.
- He wears good clothes, buys good books, drives a good car, gives generously to the poor, and has a low salary.
- He makes fifteen daily calls to parish families, visits the housebound and the hospitalized, spends all his time evangelizing the unchurched, and is always in his office when needed.
- He is very handsome.

Many pastors and Christian workers feel they are like the Chinese jugglers who spin plates on poles. They begin with four or five, and as they start each new plate, the earlier ones begin to wobble dangerously. So they dash across the stage to keep each plate spinning as it should. As one Christian worker said to me, 'I feel the only thing holding me together is perpetual motion.' If she stopped, she would collapse.

We are all familiar with the challenge of ensuring that our ministry is governed by the right priorities. The apostles in Acts 6 were very aware of the danger of being distracted from the priority tasks of the ministry of the Word and prayer. So it is wise for us to review regularly the priorities which shape our Christian service, and Paul's defence of his ministry in 2 Corinthians 4 provides us with some valuable insights as to what those priorities should be.

Contemporary challenges

It is now well known that our culture has undergone a radical shift of perspective when it comes to the issue of truth. I once spoke with a Christian student who had visited the university counsellor. She was facing some emotional difficulties, and the advice she was given was to sleep with her boyfriend. She replied that she was a Christian and she knew this would be wrong, to which the counsellor replied, 'If it's functionally helpful, then it's legitimate.' This is truth which makes no demands on us, truth that is shaped according to the patterns of our own desires and convenience. Truth has become subjective. It is true because I like it; it is true if it helps me. Truth is a commodity to be moulded to serve my ends. The inevitable result of this view is that ultimately people – and societies – lose their bearings. Morally, they become confused and bewildered. Many people are genuinely seeking a way out, looking for something which will address the uncertainty in their lives.

At the same time, we must ask whether our culture is influencing the Christian church, and influencing us as Christian leaders. To what extent is the gospel truly shaping our lives? To what extent is God's Word central to our ministry and the life of our church? In many parts of the world, the church has drifted away from these fundamental commitments. I participated not long ago in a small consultation, called by Scripture Union in response to the evident decline in Bible reading at almost all ages and all levels. In the UK, a Bible Society survey of churchgoers indicated that over half of the respondents read the Bible outside a church service just once a year. It would be true to say that our congregations will never be mature, our impact on society will never be significant, and our hopes of revival will remain distant, until we develop a stronger desire to read, understand and apply God's Word to our lives.

We must also add another challenge: the temptation to displace the centrality of Christ. There is a loss of nerve on the part of many Christians, as it becomes increasingly difficult to sustain our commitment to the uniqueness of Christ in our pluralistic age. There are suggestions from many quarters that we water down the message of Jesus Christ as Lord, Jesus Christ the Saviour of the world.

It is for these reasons that 2 Corinthians 4 is an important passage for all Christian leaders. It focuses our attention on the priority of proclaiming Christ, and of doing so with integrity. Paul faced many temptations to compromise his message and his methods. He was being criticized for a range of issues by a group of rivals in Corinth who had a very different view of leadership and apostleship. They challenged his credentials and his authority, they invaded his territory and claimed credit for his efforts, and they mocked his abilities as a preacher.

Paul, they said, was not an impressive speaker. By contrast, they displayed more dramatic signs of spirituality, they had more impressive rhetoric and far superior knowledge. There is no question that they would have come top of the perfect pastor survey. You get something of the flavour of their criticism from Paul's defence in 11:3–6.

> But I am afraid that just as Eve was deceived by the serpent's cunning, your minds may somehow be led astray from your sincere and pure devotion to Christ. For if someone comes to you and preaches a Jesus other than the Jesus we preached, or if you receive a different spirit from the one you received, or a different gospel from the one you accepted, you put up with it easily enough. But I do not think I am in the least inferior to those 'super-apostles'. I may not be a trained speaker, but I do have knowledge. We have made this perfectly clear to you in every way.

So 2 Corinthians 4 will help us understand Paul's ministry priorities; four characteristics of his ministry of the Word. They represent a fundamental aspect of our calling as leaders. Again we will find a portrait of a credible leader.

Integrity – no deception

> We have renounced secret and shameful ways; we do not use deception. (4:2)

We saw from 2 Corinthians 1 that Paul had to defend his integrity against those who accused him of being untrustworthy, of making promises but failing to deliver. Paul had replied vigorously, because he knew that acceptance of the truth of the gospel is frequently tied to the integrity of the messenger. He emphasized that his 'yes' meant 'yes'. He was reliable, and so was his message. This may be why, in chapter 4, he speaks again of his integrity with regard to that message.

'We have renounced secret and shameful ways; we do not use deception.' This is a statement about his motivation in ministry. Everything was above board. There was no attempt at cover-up. He refused to act like an unscrupulous politician, or a deceitful salesman. Unlike his opponents, Paul was completely transparent in his ministry.

I once read a political journalist's description of the Liberal Democrat party in the UK, sometimes criticized for presenting one policy one day, only to adjust the policy when speaking in a different context on another day. 'Liberal Democrats have such nice faces, even if they have two of them,' he said.

Paul underlines that he is consistent. He was not two-faced, or one thing in private and another in public. In verse 2 he continues to assert that he did not distort the message for his own purposes. He did not dilute it to make it more palatable for the audience; he did not make it conform to his particular party interests.

John Pilger recently suggested that the real first casualty of war is transparent journalism. He quoted Claud Cockburn: 'Never believe anything until it has first been officially denied.'[1] But Paul's writing was entirely trustworthy, never deceptive. A little earlier in the letter he has said the same with regard to his motives, characterized, he insists, by integrity. 'Unlike so many, we do not peddle the word of God for profit. On the contrary, in Christ we speak before God with sincerity, like men sent from God' (2:17). By implication, this group of 'pedlars' *did* pursue 'secret and shameful ways'. Such preachers, Paul suggested, tried to secure converts through deception. It is possible that they were similar to the occult groups of the day, marketing some new and mysterious religious product. Some writers think that this group objected to the way Paul spoke so openly about the gospel; they preferred the truth to be shrouded in mystery. And, of course, they could charge significant fees if people wished to benefit from their illumination of that truth. It is also possible that the word 'pedlar' originally referred to those who watered down wine for sale in the market. They were guilty of deception, but they did not care. They were salesmen whose sole motive was profit.

Paul begins with a straightforward declaration, then. He renounces any such salesmanship, any attempt to deceive his hearers, any watering down of the message. He declined financial support deliberately, to avoid having some subtle influence over them. His ministry was characterized by complete integrity.

The lessons are clear for all leaders. We might not face the temptations of serving only for financial gain, although those of us who receive our support from churches or Christian organizations need to keep alert to such a danger. But we will face the temptation to use our position to manipulate others; to present one side of the truth and not the whole; to speak about Christian conviction and behaviour, yet to live lives which are very different.

To underline the seriousness of his call and commission, Paul once again asserts that he is leading with God watching. 'We speak before God' (2:17). God is witness to his truthfulness, his sincere motivation, his integrity. He reiterates this sense of accountability. 'We commend ourselves to every man's conscience in the sight of God' (4:2). We need not explore this further, since we have spoken at length in chapter 3 about what such accountability will mean.

Fidelity – no distortion

We do not use deception, nor do we distort the word of God. On the contrary, by setting forth the truth plainly we commend ourselves to every man's conscience in the sight of God. (4:2)

Paul again underlines his determination to be faithful to the message, to tell it as it is. In the same way, we are not to distort the Word of God but present its truth plainly. To 'set forth' means an open declaration, a full disclosure of the truth. It is the opposite of deception. It means 'to show your hand'. It is like the conjuror or the magician at a circus, who rolls up his sleeves (no rabbits, only a few hairs!). So Paul insists: we are holding nothing back, we are proclaiming faithfully the whole counsel of God. And this is the force of verse 2: we do not twist the message to please our hearers, but we set forth *the truth*. We do not embellish the truth to win popularity, but we speak the message *plainly*. We do not reserve the message for an elite group, but we commend ourselves to *every man's conscience*.

In 2 Corinthians 11 we gain an insight into Paul's concern about the defective preachers in Corinth. They used familiar language, but it was another Jesus, a different spirit, a different gospel. We are not sure what this might have represented. Some writers suggest it was a gospel which majored on strength, not weakness; a message which promised triumph, not suffering. So Paul affirms his commitment to a faithful, clear, open declaration of the truth. And again we need to ask whether such fidelity is a characteristic of our own ministry. There are all kinds of temptations not to be faithful to the message – whether it be the apparent foolishness of the cross, the supposed fanaticism of declaring the uniqueness of Jesus Christ, or the charge of intellectual cowardice in being faithful to the authority of God's Word.

It will hinge, of course, on our attitude to God's revelation in Christ and in Scripture. If we believe in the unique authority of God's revelation, then we are in no position to stand above God's Word, selecting what we wish to believe and disposing of the less palatable parts. Rather, we will sit humbly beneath it, allowing its truth to fashion our thinking and behaviour. Another characteristic naturally follows.

Humility – no self-promotion

> We do not preach ourselves, but Jesus Christ as Lord, and ourselves as your servants. (4:5)

Not long ago an article appeared in *Christianity Today* which suggested that, at least in some parts of the Western world, there was emerging a consumerist attitude in the church. It was described as a 'McChurch mentality', which was pushing Christian leaders and pastors to market themselves and their church in an almost competitive spirit. It suggested that congregations approached sermons in much the same way as they approached fast-food restaurants. Today, McDonalds; tomorrow, Burger King.

In Paul's day there was certainly a problem with personality cults and a drive towards showmanship. We have already quoted them: 'In person he is unimpressive and his speaking amounts to nothing' (10:10). And Paul admits, 'I may not be a trained speaker' (11:6). His rivals in Corinth were clearly very concerned about image, about projecting themselves, their eloquence and their rhetorical skill. Paul is not afraid to confront that directly. 'We do not preach ourselves,' he asserts (4:5). We are not projecting our personalities. 'We are not trying to commend ourselves to you again' (5:12). We are not trying to build our own power base. And later in the letter, 'It is not the one who commends himself who is approved, but the one whom the Lord commends' (10:18).

He has already said this very directly in his first letter. 'When I came to you ... I did not come with eloquence or superior wisdom ... For I resolved to know nothing while I was with you except Jesus Christ and him crucified' (1 Cor. 2:1–4). And here, in 2 Corinthians 4, it is the same. 'We do not preach ourselves, but Jesus Christ as Lord.' So we notice the theological balance: in 1 Corinthians the focus is on Jesus Christ and him crucified, and here in 2 Corinthians it is on Jesus Christ as Lord. That was the essential message Paul wished to proclaim: Jesus Christ as Saviour and Lord. And he wanted nothing to get in the way of that message. That was the authoritative proclamation that really mattered. As James Denny wrote, 'Nobody has any right to preach who has not mighty affirmations to make concerning God's Son Jesus Christ – affirmations in which there is no ambiguity.'

I am sure we should feel the challenge of this text in our own leadership. In a media-conscious age it is no surprise that Christian organizations or churches look for an articulate leader with charisma, charm and conviction. In an age when Christian organizations have to work very hard to persuade churches or trusts to support them financially, it is not at all unusual to find ministries described in terms of effective leaders with powerful ministries. In an MTV age our churches can become theatres, where the performance matters more than the content, where we honour our evangelical heroes and elevate their ministries. So we should not miss the additional words of 4:5, 'and ourselves as your servants for Jesus' sake'. That was Paul's sense of identity in his leadership and in his proclamation of Jesus Christ as Lord. I am not in this for personal gain; I am not seeking glory; I am not trying to boost my ego or enhance my reputation. I am carrying out this ministry as your slave.

These verses demonstrate a powerful combination of both authority and humility. We preach Christ Jesus as Lord, and ourselves as your slaves. Leaders face the constant danger of self-promotion. They are often concerned with the issue of status, as we shall see in chapter 11. And similarly, there is a danger that churches or ministries are built around individuals, and that people join for the wrong reasons. Paul wrote in his first letter that their faith should not rest on men's wisdom but on God's power. There are, then, two vital things in verse 5: presenting Christ with faithfulness and courage, and serving others with humility. Asian evangelist and Bible teacher Ajith Fernando expresses it like this: 'I believe one of the greatest challenges facing the church in this pluralistic age is for Christians who preach the unique and authoritative gospel and also demonstrate radical servanthood.'[2]

In response to such teaching, Paul's critics would doubtless have come forward with another accusation: his preaching was ineffective. Their techniques would evoke a far bigger response. So Paul anticipates the charge.

Certainty – no illusions

> And even if our gospel is veiled, it is veiled to those who are perishing. The god of this age has blinded the minds of unbelievers, so that they cannot see the light of the gospel of the glory of Christ, who is the image of God. (4:3–4)

These verses remind us of two realities of which Paul was certain. First, *the reality of spiritual blindness*. It is possible that with the use of the words 'veil' and 'glory' Paul is making the same contrast as he made in chapter 3, where he said that the Jewish people did not really understand their own scriptures. There was a veil over their hearts and minds and the Holy Spirit was the only one who could remove it.

In the same way, now in chapter 4 he says it is true of all men and women – and we know this to be the case. There are many who are spiritually resistant. It is possible that in these verses Paul is saying that people have made this age their god, and they are blind to the truth because of such devotion. Many, however, see a reference here to Satanic influence. Jesus talks about response to the Word in his parable of the sower. 'The devil comes and takes away the word from their hearts, so that they may not believe and be saved' (Luke 8:12). We might not talk much about it in the twenty-first century, but both Paul and Jesus are direct in stating that there is such a thing as Satanic opposition to the message. There is a personal force of evil at work in the world, blinding people's minds and closing their ears. That is why our ministry of preaching and teaching, our personal sharing of the good news, our gossiping the gospel, needs also to be accompanied by our prayers for those who hear. Paul was under no illusions. Many people who hear the gospel will write it off as totally irrelevant. The gospel is effectively 'hidden' for those who are perishing, those who are losing their way (4:3). It is important to see that Paul does not underestimate the enemy, who is diligently at work 'blinding the minds of unbelievers' (4:4). All Christian ministry must be realistic at this point. There is a spiritual dimension: evangelism is not a simple marketing exercise, where we aim to overcome consumer resistance through better packaging. There is a deeper issue to which Paul refers in this passage, another certainty in our ministry.

Second, *the nature of spiritual illumination*. As he expresses it, 'For God, who said, "Let light shine out of darkness," made his light shine in our hearts to give us the light of the knowledge of the glory of God in the face of Christ' (4:6). As we do our part in proclaiming Christ Jesus as Lord, we have the assurance of God's illuminating work in the hearts and minds of people. Just as in his work of creation, so now God shines his light into their hearts to reveal the truth about Jesus. The whole passage is very Christocentric. The light that dispels the darkness of the human heart is found in the face of Jesus Christ. Paul demonstrates that the only way to know God is to know Jesus Christ. Christ, who is the image of God, is the one who reveals God's glory to us (4:4). It is only by preaching Christ, and only by the illuminating power of his Spirit, that men and women are taken out of the kingdom of darkness and into the kingdom of light. Just as Paul is realistic about the god of this age, so he is totally optimistic about the power of the message to impact people's lives.

It is much the same with Jesus' teaching in the parable of the sower to which we have already referred. The sowing metaphor is particularly potent as an illustration of Jesus' ministry and the growth of the kingdom. Sowing seems quite unimpressive; the seed is very vulnerable and there are certainly no quick results. But Jesus' ministry then and now has that kind of quality. What is the agent for change? Jesus gives the answer: 'the seed is the word of God' (Luke 8:11). It is the preaching of God's good news which will bring in God's kingdom.

We certainly need to think hard about new strategies for reaching those around us, new bridges for postmodern apologetics, new seeker-friendly environments, new creative expressions, stronger relational styles of evangelism, and much else. But the seed is the Word; the kingdom will advance only as that Word of the gospel is proclaimed and by the Spirit provokes a response in the hearts and minds of those who are ready to hear it. The gospel is the power of God to salvation for everyone who believes.

These, then, are the gospel priorities for our ministry. Our responsibility in the church may be for a small group, or for one-to-one counselling, or for youth ministry; we may be regular preachers and teachers, or care for children at home or in the church; our service may be in a busy office or hospital ward. But all of us are called to the task of faithfully presenting Jesus himself. And we are to demonstrate integrity in both the message and the method. 'For we do not preach ourselves, but Jesus Christ as Lord, and ourselves as your servants for Jesus' sake.'

Section B – Over to you . . .

- Paul indicates that he knows what it is to 'fear the Lord' as he reflects on that day when we will give an account of how we have lived. What does such godly fear mean to you?
- Do you have some key relationships that provide support and accountability at the personal level and, if not, how could you develop these relationships?
- How does a strong sense of our calling before God enable us to serve others with greater commitment?
- What are the pressures on you to displace the centrality of Christ and the authority of the Scriptures in your Christian service, and how can these priorities be guarded and maintained?

C. Leadership and community

6. Exercising authority

On a recent visit to a university education department, I noticed that a special programme was being advertised for hard-pressed teachers. It was entitled 'assertion training'. The three-week in-service training programme was designed to equip them for the daily onslaught in the classroom by projecting a more aggressive image. A similar form of training is undertaken by footballers in their pre-match warm-up as they huddle together and mutter angry words about the opposition, strengthening their communal resolve to annihilate them.

Assertion, dominance, self-assurance, self-reliance – these are the words which have often been associated with secular leadership styles. As in all areas of the Christian life, it is easy for us to be squeezed into the world's mould when thinking about the issue of leadership and authority in the church. At the same time, both within our culture and within the Christian community, there has been something of a reaction to the superstar mentality. We have become cynical about authority and uneasy about any form of hierarchy. We reject dominant leadership. There is less and less respect for politicians and the political process. Some observers suggest that the Western world faces a crisis of leadership, with fewer people ready to face the challenge of exercising leadership in the context of suspicion, cynicism and ever-present media intrusion. In such a context, exercising godly leadership within the Christian community is a demanding challenge. Exercising authority with Christian integrity is a challenge for us all. Once again, Paul provides some important lessons, this time in the closing section of the letter from chapter 10 onwards.

The change of tone in the final four chapters of the letter is so marked that commentators have varying views as to how the letter was constructed. Are these final chapters a separate letter, perhaps the 'painful letter' to which Paul referred in chapter 2? Or did Paul receive news from Corinth which impacted him so deeply that it provoked a much more assertive style of writing, warning the Corinthians about the dangers of the false apostles whose influence seemed to be ever more pervasive? Whatever the reasons, there is a marked change of mood and writing style as we enter the final chapters.

The false teachers in Corinth had certain expectations of a spiritual leader, expectations that were shaped by the Greek culture of the day. Leaders were eloquent orators, with an impressive physical presence; 'weakness' was not a word in their vocabulary. As spiritual gurus, there was also something 'otherworldly' about them; they would claim to have mystical experiences, unusual revelations, a spiritual hotline which marked them out as special. We find that Paul responds with a series of passionate arguments, each of which tells us something not only about Paul's calling as an apostle, but also about the features we should look for in all true Christian leadership.

What becomes clear throughout is that Paul is not simply protecting his touchy honour, nor concerned to defend his own reputation at all costs, but is motivated by entirely different concerns. He is deeply concerned for the welfare of the Corinthian believers, and wants to be sure that they are not captured by false notions of the gospel. His fierce response is motivated not by personal pique, but by compassion for others and a conviction that he must defend the gospel itself. And so he is speaking to two audiences: to the false teachers, and to the Corinthians as a whole. Perhaps that is why he begins in 10:1 with 'I, Paul', because it represents a statement of his authority towards the church as he prepares them for his next visit. 'By the meekness and gentleness of Christ, I appeal to you – I, Paul, who am "timid" when face to face with you, but "bold" when away!'

There are four features of true authority which appear in the first part of 2 Corinthians 10, and they are supremely relevant to Christian service of whatever kind.

The model for authority: the gentleness of Christ

Paul faced a dilemma as he confronted the charges of the false teachers. It is similar when any public figure is criticized. Politicians who face a smear campaign might well be unsure about how best to defend themselves, and Paul faced a similar situation. On the one hand, they implied that Paul was nothing other than a windbag. He was a wimp. There was nothing impressive about him, and although he tried to exercise authority in his letters, in reality he was a weakling. His bark was worse than his bite. As soon as he came face to face with them, he was 'timid' (10:1). For Paul to do nothing in the face of such accusations would only confirm the Corinthians in their suspicions: he was no apostle, he was weak-kneed and flabby, an impostor. On the other hand, to reply to such criticism with an aggressive letter would add to his troubles. 'There he goes again,' the Corinthians would say, 'writing with such "boldness", but from the safe distance of a few hundred kilometres.'

The opening words of the chapter, therefore, are especially significant. Paul's model for his leadership is Christ himself. His appeal to the Corinthians is on the basis of 'the meekness and gentleness of Christ' (10:1). It is significant that the language he uses is associated with gentleness, with Christ-like humility. The qualities with which Paul wishes to be identified are not the brash and loud-mouthed qualities of a showman, nor the manipulative oratorical skills of a politician, nor the heroic achievements of a Greek god. He wants to be identified with Jesus, with the controlled strength of the incarnate Lord.

One of the most demanding aspects of Christian leadership is facing hostile criticism. How do we respond? When we are tired, or when we have given everything for others, and our reward is anonymous hate mail through the post, it is not easy to express the meekness of Christ. It is also a good verse to reflect on whenever we engage in conflict or in theological challenges of one kind or another. What is our motivation? Is it to win people over, or is it to score points off our opponents or to boost our reputation? For many, I fear that this can be an ugly element of evangelical subculture. When some people engage in argument over the Bible, you get the feeling that, although the outward appeal is to the need to be faithful to Scripture, the manner says something very different. Gentleness is not the word for it. It is aggressive, cold, almost ruthlessly determined. It is wrapped up in the language of gospel faithfulness, but it does not truly represent the Christ of the gospel. The manner adopted by such defenders of the faith is such that it mocks the truth they are seeking to defend.

Of course, meekness and gentleness should not be taken to mean passivity. When occasion demanded, Jesus was ready for straight talking and tough action. So was Paul. Some writers suggest that the meekness of Christ he is displaying is the patient restraint from pronouncing judgment – he is giving the Corinthians one last chance to repent. (It might be similar to Peter's comment in 2 Peter 3 – delay in God's action is not the result of God's impotence, but of his mercy and patience, 'not wanting any to perish'.) Paul appeals to the Corinthians to set their house in order so that, when he next visits, he will not have to exercise as much discipline as he presently anticipates. 'I beg you that when I come I may not have to be as bold as I expect to be towards some people who think that we live by the standards of this world' (10:2). Certainly he will take bold action if this is needed. 'We will be ready to punish every act of disobedience' (10:6). But his style is not like that of the false teachers.

Whatever our responsibility in the Christian community, our approach to others should be modelled on the meekness and gentleness of Christ. Whether in situations of disagreement, or in the demanding exercise of church discipline, such Christ-like humility should always govern the style and manner of our service.

The foundation for exercising authority: the gospel of Christ

In several of his letters Paul mentions that Christians are equipped for spiritual warfare with the weapons which God supplies. They include the truth of the gospel, the Word of God, prayer and faith, all empowered by the Holy Spirit. Here Paul describes such weapons as powerful and effective (10:4). They demolish strongholds – perhaps an echo of Proverbs 21:22, 'A wise man attacks the city of the mighty and pulls down the stronghold in which they trust.'

The language he uses in this section leads us to conclude that Paul is especially concerned about the ideological battle, the battle for hearts and minds. He is concerned to demonstrate to the false teachers that the wisdom of this world is foolishness, and that true apostleship is not founded on human wisdom or intellectual pretension, but on the gospel of Christ. He says much the same in 1 Corinthians 1: 'Where is the wise man? Where is the scholar? Where is the philosopher of this age? Has not God made foolish the wisdom of the world? . . . God was pleased through the foolishness of what was preached to save those who believe (1:20, 21).

The real issue is to do with the gospel itself. We will overcome these enemies of truth by a clear presentation of the gospel. 'We demolish arguments and every pretension that sets itself up against the knowledge of God, and we take captive every thought to make it obedient to Christ' (10:5). The message of the gospel is able to demolish those strongholds that resist Christ's rule, and so Paul's purpose is to take captive every thought for obedience to Christ. That was the problem with the false teachers: they were refusing to submit in obedience to Christ (10:6). Our task is serious and demanding: it is to demolish arguments and take captive every thought by proclaiming Jesus crucified and risen, and to do so by also embodying that message. It is not simply intellectual warfare. By the power of the gospel and the Spirit, true spiritual warfare is to confront every obstacle that will prevent total allegiance to Jesus Christ.

Integrity in our leadership will therefore mean a firm commitment to the truth of God's Word. I am slightly nervous of using the language of warfare, for reasons which I have already touched on. It should not be taken to imply aggression, for we have already noted the language of meekness and gentleness. That is the whole point of Paul's defence: we are not to 'wage war as the world does'. As leaders we refuse to use the tactics of intimidation, or the force of personality, or the threats of violence. We live by entirely different standards and serve others by entirely different values.

Nevertheless, warfare language is here in 2 Corinthians, and for good reason. Christian ministry is gospel-centred, and there will be many times when we must ensure that every aspect of our work is rooted in the truth of God's Word. We saw this as we looked at Paul's gospel priorities in 2 Corinthians 4, and here again we see its significance. Any authority we exercise should arise from the authority of the gospel.

The purpose of authority: building up the body of Christ

> For even if I boast somewhat freely about the authority the Lord gave us for building you up rather than pulling you down, I will not be ashamed of it. (10:8)

Paul next outlines the foundation for his apostleship. He is not afraid of his apostleship being tested, but he is concerned to establish the right criteria for such a test. First, like all true believers, he belongs to Christ: 'If anyone is confident that he belongs to Christ, he should consider again that we belong to Christ just as much as he' (10:7). If some in Corinth were parading their spiritual credentials, they should remember that Paul had met the risen Christ, and that he had been called and commissioned by him, as he has explained so fully in earlier parts of the letter. Not only that, as we saw in chapter 4, he was their spiritual father and therefore had God-given authority amongst them.

But why had he been given that authority? It was not for the purpose of destroying them, but for strengthening them.

Paul says the same in chapter 13: 'the authority the Lord gave me for building you up, not for tearing you down' (13:10). Even what appear to be harsh words are motivated by a desire to be constructive. And Paul is anxious not to be misunderstood. The apparently harsh rebukes which he has to issue are not to frighten them (10:9), but to strengthen them (10:8). The fatherly discipline which he has to introduce is a necessary corrective if they are to be true to the gospel.

Again, this is extremely good advice for us. Whatever our sphere of Christian service, our calling is to encourage and strengthen others. The exercise of our gifts is not to boost our ego or impress the crowds, but to build one another up. We will look at this in more detail in the next chapter.

The context of authority: a life like Christ's

Paul adds one further feature of the exercise of his authority which we have been highlighting throughout the book. He acts with complete integrity. Although he is accused of being one thing on paper and another in person (10:10), he insists that he is completely consistent. What he says, he will do: 'Such people should realise that what we are in our letters when we are absent, we will be in our actions when we are present' (10:11). He will discipline those who need it, and punish disobedience if that is required (10:6).

In 2 Corinthians 11 he will respond more directly to the suggestion that 'he is unimpressive and his speaking amounts to nothing' (10:10). These accusations were part of the whispering campaign against Paul that was clearly gathering momentum in Corinth. The Christians were in danger of believing the hype of the 'super-apostles', whose view of Christian leadership owed more to secular models than to Christ.

This is one of the reasons why this section of the letter is especially valuable to us. In our world, Christian leaders can be tempted to build their reputation and shape their style on the superficial expectations of today's culture. Instead of the meekness and gentleness of Christ, they become dictators, 'little tin gods' as J. B. Phillips once expressed it. Instead of using the weapons of gospel truth, they rely on the force of personality, the glitz of the showman, or the manipulative oratory of a salesman. Instead of building up their fellow believers, they become authoritarian, lacking the humility which characterizes a servant of Christ. And their lives lack the fundamental integrity of deeds matching words.

This section represents Paul's opening volley in a sustained attack on the false apostles, but he has demonstrated the qualities which all true servants of the Lord should emulate: a commitment to the gentleness of Christ, the gospel of Christ, the body of Christ and the life of Christ.

7. Building community

Some years ago I took up a pastoral appointment in a church, and on my first Sunday an older Christian came up to me and offered me a word of encouragement. 'God's people will break your heart,' he said. Hardly what I wanted to hear on day one, but I discovered that it was realistic advice. Anyone called into Christian leadership, of whatever kind, realizes soon enough that from time to time their motives will be questioned, their judgment will be doubted, their words viewed with suspicion. Rather tough on the Christian community, you think? Well, perhaps. But you do not need to talk to many congregations, let alone church leaders, to discover that the church is a human institution as well as a divine one. Like any family, it has its struggles but also its many compensating joys. It is God's purpose that, through the rough and tumble of Christian community, we should grow together in Christian maturity. Leading with integrity is a wonderful challenge, and in this chapter we will range a little across 2 Corinthians to note several features of leading in community.

Leadership that strengthens others
Despite the rocky relationship Paul had with the Corinthians, we have already noted in chapter 4 that this remained his primary focus: 'All this is for your benefit' (4:15).

- 'For even if I boast somewhat freely about the authority the Lord gave us for building you up rather than pulling you down, I am not ashamed of it.' (10:8)
- 'Have you been thinking all along that we have been defending ourselves to you? We have been speaking in the sight of God as those in Christ; and everything we do, dear friends, is for your strengthening.' (12:19)
- 'This why I write these things when I am absent, that when I come I may not have to be harsh in my use of authority – the authority the Lord gave me for building you up, not for tearing you down.' (13:10)

His concern was for their restoration. The purpose of his ministry as an apostle was to see them mature. His concern is entirely for their strengthening, and this theme echoes through Paul's writing.[1] True Christian leadership seeks the well-being of others, and one of the greatest joys is to see others making progress. If the group or congregation for which you are responsible is developing in a healthy way, maturing in its relationships and achieving its purpose, then there can be few greater rewards for the leader.

Leaders with integrity see this as a primary goal. We have already seen that the focus of leadership is service – our service for Christ and the service of others. That has the primary intention of equipping others to fulfil their calling. Our first concern should not be personal recognition or the praise of admiring crowds, but the growth of those whom we are called to serve. Leadership gifts in the church are given precisely for this purpose: 'to prepare God's people for works of service, so that the body of Christ may be built up' (Eph. 4:12).

As we have seen, however, the task of helping the Corinthians was fraught with difficulty and not a little personal pain. Nevertheless, Paul was determined not to shrink from the task of his pastoral and apostolic duty. How would he go about strengthening others?

Leadership that encourages transparency

> We have spoken freely to you, Corinthians, and opened wide our hearts
> to you. We are not withholding our affection from you, but you are
> withholding yours from us. As a fair exchange – I speak as to my
> children – open wide your hearts also. (6:11–13)

The most challenging arena in which Christian integrity is tested is in our relationships. Paul had taken his fellow believers into his trust, exposing his frailties and vulnerabilities as he described the hardships of his service for them and for the Lord. And as he faces the awkwardness of the relationship with them, he demonstrates two qualities which need to be held together.

First, honesty. 'We have spoken freely to you, Corinthians' (6:11). Using their name in this verse heightens the sense of emotional intensity. He has opened his heart to them, he has held nothing back, and he longs that they should do the same towards him. 'As a fair exchange – I speak as to my children – open wide your hearts also' (6:13). He picks this up again in 7:2, appealing as a father to his children, longing for open hearts and open communication. Part of Paul's appeal would have included a call to reject the rival gospel offered by the so-called leaders in Corinth. 'Don't go back on the message I brought to you, don't reject me or reject the truth of the gospel.' Sometimes we are not too good at 'speaking freely'. Either we confront people in a strongly assertive way, or we tell everyone else about the problem, other than the person to whom we really should be talking. But Paul's open attitude and honest speaking is complemented by another quality.

Second, affection. 'We are not withholding our affection from you, but you are withholding yours from us' (6:12). There are few things which are more painful than love which is spurned. Paul was expressing his affection towards them, openly describing his thoughts and feelings, yet they appeared to be maintaining a cool indifference. 'Make room for us in your hearts,' he appeals (7:2). He clearly felt they had slammed the door, and he felt it keenly because of his deep affection for believers who were being seduced by the rival teachers.

One of the characteristics of genuine Christian fellowship in our churches or organizations will be open hearts. We can usually tell that this is a feature of a healthy community by such practical signs as open homes, not formal relationships; open fellowship, not special in-groups; open communication which confronts as well as encourages, not innuendo and gossip. In the last few years I have found myself in three different contexts where I and others have had to learn to confront in a godly way; not to sweep things under the carpet, not to complain to other people, but to address issues firmly and compassionately. I have not found this easy – partly because of my temperament, my British reserve, and my natural desire to avoid uncomfortable and unpredictable situations. That is why these verses are so helpful in their combination of qualities: it is both speaking freely *and* with much affection. Opening our hearts wide is an essential part of Christian integrity and represents an attractive feature of Christian community which commends the gospel in an age of fractured relationships.

Transparency, of course, is not only required when confronting challenges of the kind Paul is discussing. It is a basic quality that arises from a truly integrated life. We are who we are. 'What we are is plain to God, and I hope it is also plain to your conscience' (5:11). It is the opposite of the deceptive behaviour of the super-apostles in town, whom Paul describes as Satan's servants who 'masquerade as servants of righteousness' (11:14).

In his highly popular books, Daniel Goleman speaks a good deal about emotional intelligence and self-management. Leaders need personal as well as social competence, with the discipline to manage themselves as well as to manage their relationships. In writing about the 'neuroanatomy of leadership', he lists transparency as a leadership virtue and an organizational strength.

> Transparency – an authentic openness to others about one's feelings, beliefs and actions – allows integrity, or the sense that a leader can be trusted. At a primal level, integrity hinges on impulse control, keeping us from acting in ways that we might regret. Integrity also means that a leader lives his values. Such leaders strike others as genuine because they are not making a pretense of being other than they are. Integrity, therefore, boils down to one question: Is what you're doing in keeping with your own values?[2]

I like the emphasis very much, except that, when it comes to self-management, I tend to respond like Paul: 'I have the desire to do what is good, but I cannot carry it out' (Rom. 7:18). What a wonderful thing that Paul continues in Romans 8:9: 'You, however, are controlled not by the sinful nature but by the Spirit, if the Spirit of God lives in you.'

Leadership that creates trust
Transparency is closely related to the theme of trustworthiness. Most writers on the subject of leadership see trust as the essential foundation. It is not developed overnight, but earned over an extended period of credible behaviour. Trust is given to leaders who live with integrity. Their job is to nurture that same atmosphere within the community.

In his Temple Address in October 2004, Clive Mather, President and CEO of Shell Canada, said, 'Trust is essential to the running of markets. As Alan Greenspan, [recent] Chairman of the Federal Reserve pointed out, even when followed to the letter, rules guide only a few of the day-to-day decisions required of business and financial managers. The rest are governed by whatever personal code of values that managers bring to the table. So the key question is not whether the contract is watertight but can I trust this person and their values.'[3]

In the UK the Evangelical Alliance has urged Christian leaders to reflect on the MORI survey which showed that, while 91% of the British public trusts doctors to tell the truth (compared with 87% for teachers, 74% for professors, 72% for judges), it indicated continuing decline in trust for church leaders. Clergy come in at 70%, but, as David Hilborn of the EA reported, trust in the church as an institution seems to be plummeting. In the 1990 European Values Survey, only 43% of people trust the church, with just 30% of 18–24-year-olds doing so. Christian leaders have to confront this drift. Not only does it seriously impair the functioning of the body of Christ, it seriously impacts our mission.

Paul provides the Corinthians with a very simple apologetic in his response to criticism. 'We have wronged no one, we have corrupted no one, we have exploited no one . . . I have great confidence in you; I take great pride in you. I am greatly encouraged; in all our troubles my joy knows no bounds' (7:2, 4). It has been suggested that the three verbs ('wronged', 'corrupted', 'exploited') were commonly used of wrongful financial activities, but there is probably wider application.

- 'We have wronged no one': there is nothing in our relationship with others which is inappropriate, unjust or unloving.
- 'We have corrupted no one': we have not abused our position, whether in our relationship with those of the opposite sex, in tactics of intimidation, or in our handling of the truth of the gospel.[4]
- 'We have exploited no one': here Paul is probably answering the charge that, although he refused financial support, he has had his hand in the till all along, taking a cut from the offering which Titus was administering (12:17–18). The false teachers were certainly guilty of that, Paul suggests (11:20). But Paul has already stated that 'we do not peddle the word of God for profit' (2:17).

While Paul's writing is specific to a particular set of challenging relationships and demanding circumstances, there is much to reflect on when it comes to our own Christian service. Wronged – corrupted – exploited: they are words which can characterize leadership that lacks integrity. I once had the sad duty of trying to resolve a situation in a Christian organization where the behaviour of the senior staff member was so robust that staff in his care referred to it as 'bullying'. Looking back on the situation, I now see that much, if not all, of his behaviour was unintentional; it certainly was not intended to be destructive, for he was a warm-hearted believer. Yet the force of his personality was such that fellow workers felt intimidated. And little by little, as trust was eroded, their sense of community was lost. It became too difficult for them to work together. So we must always nurture our working relationships with sensitivity and compassion, building trust at every opportunity.

Paul also adds a strong affirmation of loyalty in the same chapter, 2 Corinthians 7. The Corinthians matter deeply to him. He builds trust with the encouragements of verse 4: 'I have great confidence in you; I take great pride in you.' While he was ready to confront the Corinthians directly, he did not criticize them in front of others – not even Titus, whom he commissioned as the messenger. How did he describe the Corinthians? There was no sense of bitterness or criticism, but rather expressions of pride and confidence in them. 'I had boasted to him about you, and you have not embarrassed me. But just as everything we said to you was true, so our boasting about you to Titus has proved to be true as well ... I am glad I can have complete confidence in you' (7:14, 16).

Although Paul had the opportunity to blacken the Corinthians' character as he briefed Titus, he refused to follow that route. He boasted of his confidence in them, and engaged in the vital ministry of encouragement. Since they had responded with godly sorrow (7:11), he is strong in his affirmations of them, positive about their fellowship and open about his depth of joy.

- 'I take great pride in you. I am greatly encouraged.' (7:4)
- '... my joy was greater than ever.' (7:7)
- 'By all this we are encouraged.' (7:13)
- 'I am glad I can have complete confidence in you.' (7:16)

Titus was caught up in the same spirit of affirmation and joy. Initially fearful of meeting the Corinthians, he had been warmly received and his own spirit had been refreshed through the visit (7:13, 15). Paul's sense of joy did not come from having scored the points and won the battle. It was the joy of fellowship restored, of the triumph of the gospel of grace and reconciliation.

In all situations our task is to encourage a sense of mutual joy, interdependence and loyalty to one another. We must ourselves be trustworthy, and work with others to create a spirit of trustworthiness in the fellowships to which we belong.

Leadership that stimulates teamwork

> Not that we lord it over your faith, but we work with you for your joy, because it is by faith you stand firm. (1:24)

The literature of leadership and management today is focusing more and more on team approaches and participative styles of various kinds. This makes sense in any institution, secular or Christian, because it is biblical – and it is a vital ingredient in our leading with integrity.

I once saw an inspirational poster in an office: 'Teamwork – means never having to take all the blame yourself.' But there are more positive reasons than this! We have seen the context of 2 Corinthians 1. The severe letter Paul wrote was painful for everyone concerned, Paul included. He had cancelled his visit because he felt the emotional demands would be too great for everyone. It was because of his deep love for them that he wrote the letter, and because of his love that he postponed his visit.

There are two features we should highlight in relation to our theme, both of which appear in 1:24. They arise from the relational qualities that Paul demonstrated, even in this demanding context of ill-feeling and mistrust, and they are vital ingredients in effective team leadership.

First, notice Paul's comment in verse 24: 'Not that we lord it over your faith . . .' His leadership style was one that respected those with whom he worked. He was no tyrant. He and his team of workers were not lords or rulers over them or over any other Christian community. We have seen this in 4:5, 'For we do not preach ourselves, but Jesus Christ as Lord, and ourselves as your servants for Jesus' sake.' 'Jesus is Lord,' Paul says, 'and I will do nothing to take his place in your life.' Here Paul was following the instructions of Jesus himself. Luke records the dispute amongst the disciples about who was the greatest. Jesus said to them, 'The kings of the Gentiles lord it over them; and those who exercise authority over them call themselves Benefactors. But you are not to be like that. Instead, the greatest among you should be like the youngest, and the one who rules like the one who serves' (Luke 22:25–26).

Or Peter: 'not greedy for money, but eager to serve; not lording it over those entrusted to you, but being examples to the flock' (1 Pet. 5:2–3).

It is true that authentic Christian ministry is founded on biblical authority, as we have seen in chapter 5. But this should never lead to *authoritarianism*. We do not impose our will. Apparently Paul's opponents did not hesitate to do so. For example, there is an intriguing reference to the Corinthians welcoming travelling preachers who dominated, and by force of personality bullied them around. 'In fact, you even put up with anyone who enslaves you or exploits you or takes advantage of you or pushes himself forward or slaps you in the face' (11:20). Such preachers proclaimed themselves as 'lord'. But Paul refused the common manipulative techniques of his day. He did not fit the first-century model of a leader.

So how does Paul operate? 'Not that we lord it over your faith, but we *work with you* for your joy' (1:24, my italics). There is equality and mutuality. If we use the phrase 'working with you' to define his style of leadership, then we can say it was 'synergetic' not 'autocratic'. It was working *with and alongside others*, not ruling over them. Paul was someone committed to teamwork. He worked closely with colleagues in his team; he laboured alongside fellow workers in the churches; even as an apostle he refused to stand on his dignity.

Mutuality is also a feature of Paul's leadership elsewhere in the letter. Paul asserts that he is not interested in party politics amongst Christians – there should be no rivalry, no pride, no taking credit for the work done by others (10:12–16).

While I am aware that there are often severe financial challenges in our churches and organizations which make plurality and collegiality difficult, we should be concerned that the model of leadership which is shaped by a solo pastor or a solo leader can at times be a dangerously vulnerable one. It is likely that too many decisions, and too much responsibility and authority, fall on the shoulders of one person, and this is not supported in Scripture. There is a need for support, for accountability, for collegiality. Even when churches cannot afford paid staff, every effort must be made to ensure that there is team leadership, shared responsibility, mutual accountability. We cannot expect the church to function as a biblical community if its leadership is not modelling this kind of teamwork. Similarly, we cannot expect a church congregation to function as an effective team if we as leaders fail to model a true commitment to working with others. This will mean, as Ajith Fernando comments, laying aside our 'messiah complexes' and recognizing our need of others. When I read the book *Leadership is an Art* by Max DePree, I was struck by the wisdom of the opening sentence: that one of the primary responsibilities of the leader is to say thank you.[5] That is, the leader acknowledges his dependence on others.

Paul knew this well enough. We have seen from 2 Corinthians 7 that he was under considerable pressure ('conflicts on the outside, fears within', 7:5). But he was comforted by his good friend Titus, and by the news of the warm response towards him of the Corinthians themselves (7:7).

The New Testament theologian Fred Bruce comments in his book about the Pauline circle that there are about seventy people mentioned by name in the New Testament of whom we would never have heard were it not for their association with Paul. Then on top of that there were many unnamed friends. His list of friends (and a few opponents) in 2 Timothy 4, to which we have already referred, represents an important aspect of his leadership legacy. His life was coming to an end, and his thoughts went to his fellow workers, who had not only provided personal support but had extended the mission way beyond what Paul alone could have achieved.

Such genuine partnership with others is the way to ensure that we live our lives with integrity. 'Once we allow ourselves to minister *under* God, not *as* God, we will be able to open the door to those who want to build friendships with us, recognising our need for the support friends can bring to us.'[6]

Leadership that lives the life

A short while ago, a 22-year-old Scout troop leader crashed into a parked car as she was leaving a Scout meeting in Great Lumley,

County Durham. It caused only minor damage, but she left false details under the windscreen of the Volvo she had hit, and then sent text messages to two Scouts she was taking home, asking them to say that no accident had taken place. A judge at Durham Crown Court told her, 'I fear your future with the Scouts is uncertain. You don't, in my view, portray the right example to be leading Scouts.' We can understand the reasons for his recommendation that she be removed from office. The Scout law includes such affirmations as, 'A Scout is to be trusted; a Scout is loyal; a Scout has courage in all difficulties; a Scout makes good use of time and is careful of possessions and property; a Scout has self-respect and respect for others.'[7]

We know that our lives are being watched. And we know that this is one of the ways in which people learn. Paul was aware of the principle, and could even say to the Corinthians, 'Follow my example, as I follow the example of Christ' (1 Cor. 11:1). It was also why he was so concerned to avoid the opposite influence: 'We put no stumbling-block in anyone's path, so that our ministry will not be discredited. Rather, as servants of God we commend ourselves in every way' (2 Cor. 6:3).

- 'Set them an example by doing what is good. In your teaching show integrity, seriousness and soundness of speech that cannot be condemned, so that those who oppose you may be ashamed because they have nothing bad to say about us.' (Titus 2:7–8)
- 'You are witnesses, and so is God, of how holy, righteous and blameless we were among you who believed.' (1 Thess. 2:10)

Paul piles up the adverbs in a dramatic way – holy, righteous, blameless. This was at the heart of his ministry – and godly example can be an enormously influential ingredient in a healthy church. As we often comment, Christian character is as much caught as taught. And not only that: Paul states that this also shaped his pastoral ministry. Like a father he encouraged, comforted and urged those believers 'to live lives worthy of God' (1 Thess. 2:11), to follow his example.

We learn best by being alongside godly believers. Whether in the more formal mentoring relationships, or in the ministry of encouragement and coaching, it is of vital importance in Christian ministry that we ensure our lives are truly modelling the truth of the gospel. Like parents, we should be giving energy to the shaping and forming of others through encouragement supported by practical and genuine example.

In 1 Thessalonians it is worth noting one other element of example. One of the most obvious features of chapter 1 is the sequence that Paul describes – the chain reaction:

- 'our gospel came to you' (v. 5);
- 'you welcomed the message' (v. 6);
- 'The Lord's message rang out from you . . . everywhere' (v. 8).

The same ripple effect is described in terms of modelling and emulating:

- 'You became imitators of us' (v. 6);
- 'you became a model to all the believers in Macedonia and Achaia' (v. 7).

From the seaport of Thessalonica the message rippled out, echoing around the mountains, spreading far and wide, and it was not just a message, but a model. People heard about the impact of the gospel on the church. So the integrity of their Christian lives had a profound impact, a ripple effect not only on surrounding cities and provinces, but across time and generations: 'your faith in God has become known everywhere' (1:8). The building up of Christian community and the advance of the gospel in our day will be through those who both speak and live the gospel.

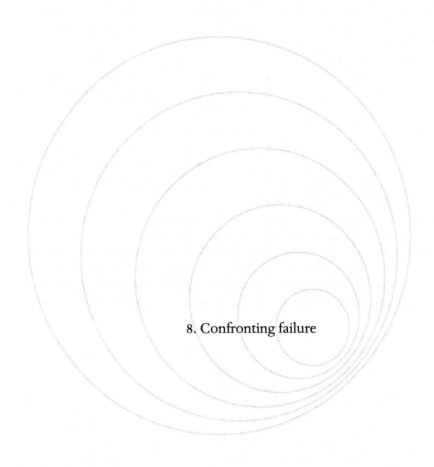

8. Confronting failure

Whenever we talk about community, we must talk about conflict. Realistically, the two belong together. We can understand the logic: community means diversity, diversity means difference, and difference often means conflict. 'It is no exaggeration to say that where two or three are gathered in Jesus' name ... then there is almost bound to be conflict at one time or another,' says Paul Beasley-Murray.[1]

Some argue that conflict is an essential element of the well-being of an organization, creating the necessary creative tensions for growth and avoiding the passivity and indifference which stifle it. That is positive thinking, of course, because we could recount many stories of conflict that can be destructive. Thankfully, Paul's experience with the Corinthians is not one of them. Certainly he and they knew something of the pain of conflict, but the story has significant lessons about how conflict and failure can be redeemed for God's good purposes when handled with integrity.

Before we come to a specific issue in Paul's correspondence with the Corinthians, it is important to note that the whole letter relates to the wider issue of Paul's relationship with them. Indeed, one substantial volume on the Corinthian correspondence has the title *Conflict and Community in Corinth*. It is worth quoting the author, Ben Witherington, because he demonstrates how much is at stake:

> Paul focuses considerable attention on addressing and trying to
> overcome specific obstacles in the way of full reconciliation with his
> spiritual children ... Paul believed that failure to achieve this
> reconciliation would endanger the very Christian identity of the
> Corinthian *ekklesia*, since Paul was Christ's agent. To be alienated
> from the agent was to be alienated from the one who sent him.
> So not only the integrity of Paul's ministry but also the integrity of the
> Corinthian's faith is at stake. Paul must defend himself, his behavior,
> and his ministry and he must also protect his converts from the very
> real danger of apostasy. The letter thus attempts to put into practice
> what Paul so eloquently preaches in 5:17–19. If Paul is the ambassador
> of reconciliation between God in Christ and the Corinthians, to discredit
> the ambassador is to deny the reality of the Corinthian's reconciliation
> to God.[2]

Within the demanding relationship between Paul and the Corinthians, however, there is reference to a situation of failure from which we can draw some key lessons. Paul introduces the issue:

> If anyone has caused grief, he has not so much grieved me as he has grieved all of you, to some extent – not to put it too severely. The punishment inflicted on him by the majority is sufficient for him. Now instead, you ought to forgive and comfort him, so that he will not be overwhelmed by excessive sorrow. I urge you, therefore, to reaffirm your love for him. (2 Cor. 2:5–8)

The word 'discipline' is not so common in the vocabulary of today's church. The mood of our age, which stresses tolerance and steers clear of judgment or the allocation of blame, has so influenced us that the thought of disciplining fellow Christians seems strangely out of place today. These verses demonstrate how Paul handled a specific case of failure. Far from being uncaring and dictatorial, Paul demonstrates his integrity not only in the way he confronts the Corinthians, but also in his attitude to a particular offender.

Integrity in our response to injury

'Pastors are among the angriest people I work with,' says A. D. Hart.[3] Handling failure in relationships is one of the most demanding tests of our leadership. It becomes even more acute when the failure relates to our own personal injury. In 2:6 Paul refers to the punishment that had been inflicted on a member of the congregation. Although it is possible that this is a reference to the same person whom Paul describes in 1 Corinthians 5 (an immoral brother who had to be expelled from the congregation), it is much more likely that it is a description of someone in the Corinthian church who had offended Paul in some way. The offender had caused grief for Paul, probably in the form of a public insult, and this not only offended Paul but had wider repercussions.

We know that failure always has a corporate impact. It can affect our family, our fellow workers and even the wider church. Because the Christian community is one body, the failure of one person affects the entire community. Although it seems as though the offence was directed towards Paul, he indicates that such a failure will have grieved all of them (2:5). An injury inflicted on one person will result in pain being widely felt. There is a domino effect, and that is one of the reasons why discipline is necessary.

But the lesson in integrity is seen in Paul's response to this injury. The Corinthians had disciplined the offender (7:6–13), but Paul was concerned that the matter should be brought to closure with both firmness and forgiveness. Enough was enough. Paul was not given to vindictiveness. He knew that discipline had its purpose, but once this was achieved, the time had come for generous forgiveness and restoration.

I am impressed by his response, because I understand why A. D. Hart discovered so much anger amongst Christian leaders. We have served others with sacrificial commitment, our families have taken the strain with us, we have worked long hours for relatively meagre financial rewards, and we feel tired and overburdened. Then a member of our team or a person in the church inflicts an injury upon us or our family. That is the time when some leaders explode with anger. The meekness and gentleness of Christ, which we have suggested is a mark of godly leadership, would not describe our attitude and maybe not our actions.

So it is impressive to hear Paul call time: you must forgive him, as I have done. In fact, he almost seems to have forgotten the offence: 'If you have forgiven anyone, I also forgive him. And what I have forgiven – if there was anything to forgive – I have forgiven in the sight of Christ for your sake' (2:10). Tom Wright comments on the liberating effect of this kind of response.

'What can I do for you, then?' The doctor smiled over his spectacles.
    'It's my memory', said the patient. 'I just can't remember things like I used to.'
    'How long has this problem being going on?' asked the doctor.
    The patient looked puzzled.
    'What problem?' he replied.
    It is one of the core disciplines of the Christian life that, with certain things, we should intend to forget them, and succeed . . . 'Whatever I've forgiven', he begins, and then racks his brain to see if he has in fact forgiven anyone anything. He assumes he must have done, but he can't for the life of him think who or what it is.

'If indeed I have forgiven anyone anything.' This isn't absent-mindedness. It is part of a rigorous self-discipline. When Paul forgives, he also forgets.[4]

We may not always be able to get that far, although it is wise encouragement. If we find it hard to lay aside personal injury, there is a further strategy to adopt which will enable us to respond with integrity. We have already referred in chapter 2 to one of Paul's opponents listed in 2 Timothy 4: 'Alexander the metalworker did me a great deal of harm. The Lord will repay him for what he has done. You too should be on your guard against him, because he strongly opposed our message' (vv. 14–15). Paul was not vindictive. He did not seek vengeance. There are no threats or angry words. Instead, he states, 'The Lord will repay him . . .' Here Paul follows the example of Christ, who 'entrusted himself to him who judges justly' (1 Pet. 2:23).

The point is strengthened as he describes his sense of isolation. 'Do your best to come to me quickly, for Demas, because he loved this world, has deserted me and has gone to Thessalonica' (2 Tim. 4:9–10). The loss of Demas would have been very painful for Paul. Demas was a close fellow worker, often associated with Paul and Luke. He would have been in a position of trust. But 'he loved the world', and he had deserted Paul. Worse still, Paul continues, 'At my first defence, no one came to my support, but everyone deserted me. May it not be held against them' (v. 16). The final phrase reflects a Christ-like generosity as he indicates he wishes them no harm. It is all the more impressive when we consider the desperate circumstances in which Paul finds himself. Deserted, opposed, unsupported, imprisoned, freezing cold, facing the death sentence – but 'may it not be held against them'.

It is true that we are forgiven by God's grace, but we have seen from 2 Corinthians 5 that we are also responsible to the Lord, the Judge, to whom we must give an account of how we have lived – our attitudes, choices, words and actions. So this should inspire us to respond to injury not with anger, not holding grudges or nurturing ill-feeling towards fellow Christians, but with the meekness of Christ. 'I have forgiven in the sight of Christ' (2 Cor. 2:10).

Integrity in appropriate discipline

The punishment inflicted on him by the majority is sufficient for him . . . The reason I wrote to you was to see if you would stand the test and be obedient in everything. (2:6, 9)

The word Paul uses for the discipline that had been exercised is 'punishment', and this is related to the word 'rebuke'. It was important that the Corinthians took heed of Paul's 'severe letter' and that they acted as he requested. It was an expression of their obedience to the apostle and therefore their obedience to God (2:9). But Paul is now writing to indicate that sufficient discipline has been exercised. All discipline needs to be appropriate to the offence, neither too lenient nor too severe. If it is overdone it can be counterproductive, producing not just 'excessive sorrow' but sometimes further defection.

Issiaka Coulbalu writes on these verses from an African perspective, but the comments have global relevance.

In too many Christian communities in Africa, discipline is abused by ethnic groups and individuals. They use it for retaliation, judgement and condemnation, rather than as an opportunity for a member to repent and abandon his or her sin permanently. Rather than removing sin, such discipline unfortunately provides an opportunity for it to grow and sets brothers and sisters against one another.[5]

It happens in every culture. Because Paul is concerned to avoid such consequences, he deliberately stresses that his forgiveness and theirs is essential, 'in order that Satan might not outwit us' (2:11). Satan is not passive when it comes to relational breakdown or community fracture. He will often be behind its inception, and he will want to deepen and extend its impact. We need to be alert to his schemes and be ready, through forgiveness and acceptance, to restore the person who has fallen so that no further spiritual injury is inflicted on the Christian community. Discipline must be carried out with integrity and with wisdom. Its purpose is to call for repentance and to encourage restoration and reconciliation. This must be uppermost in our minds as we care for those who fall. It is not hard to do this if we realize that we too are in need of God's grace.

Integrity in generous forgiveness

As we have seen, Paul was ready to forgive the personal injury, and he urges the Christian community not only to do the same, but to reaffirm their love for the offender. We can all understand why this is necessary. I have just spoken with a friend who had to endure the pain of a public rebuke before many of her colleagues, and she described the agonies associated with the sense of isolation which that produced. Perhaps you have had the experience in your family or in the church of being confronted with your failure. Whatever the initial problem that calls for discipline, we immediately feel 'outside'; we feel condemned by others. We need to know the forgiveness of God, but also the forgiveness of our fellow believers (2:7). But more than that – we also need to feel that we belong. We need their comfort and the positive reaffirmation of their love for us (2:7–8).

What is especially significant here, however, is the way Paul takes the lead in demonstrating what needs to be done. He is careful to demonstrate his own willingness to forgive alongside his call that they should forgive the offender. There is a genuineness about his response, since once again he indicates that he does so 'in the sight of Christ'. He recognizes that he lives his life in Christ's presence and therefore must be completely genuine in all his attitudes and actions. In the most challenging context of personal pain and demanding forgiveness, he is leading with God watching.

I had a difficult time a few years ago. I felt I was treated poorly by another Christian leader. It inevitably impacted my work, affected my wife, and began to drain me emotionally. It was at times a struggle to retain my integrity: not to harbour the wrong kind of thoughts, or speak inappropriately about the person in conversation with others. It took me some months finally to be able to lay the matter aside, and to pick up the relationship once again with forgiveness, openness and generosity. It was God's grace that enabled me to do this, expressed through the support of good friends who helped restore my perspective. It is never easy, but integrity calls us to demonstrate forgiveness and to reject any personal vindictiveness. Paul refused to harbour such an attitude; he called for appropriate, but not excessive, discipline. He urged forgiveness and modelled a generous spirit. Peter Brain summarizes the attitudes and actions we need:

- I will not raise the matter again;
- I will not tell others about it;
- I will not dwell on the matter myself.[6]

Recovering integrity

While the theme we have been addressing has related to how we handle the failures of others, it is necessary to confront our own failure too. A book about integrity is well and good, but many of us feel we do not match up. We may have failed in a very public way, and may wonder if there will ever be a pathway back to Christian service. Or we may be aware of the multiple inconsistencies of our lives and the hypocrisy of our leadership.

In such circumstances, we begin where Paul began. 'Therefore, since through God's mercy we have this ministry, we do not lose heart' (2 Cor. 4:1). Paul the violent persecutor of the church, Paul the blasphemer, was now an apostle by God's mercy. All of us stand on that ground. None of us can speak of Christian ministry, leadership or integrity without also affirming that 'the grace of our Lord was poured out on me abundantly, along with the faith and love that are in Christ Jesus' (1 Tim. 1:13–14). This is where our ministry begins, how it continues, and where it ends. Our calling to serve the Lord is a calling of his grace and mercy.

Then we should also see that integrity is shaped through the process of failure that is handled in the light of God's grace. In writing about the crisis of leadership, Walter Wright suggests that it arises from a crisis of forgiveness. 'Leaders are expected to lead without mistakes. There is very little tolerance for error in our organisations, very little acknowledgement of the human limitations of leaders.'[7] Churches and organizations would do well to remember that leaders grow when they are given the space to fail and the opportunity to learn. This is where supportive teamwork is so essential. But failure, of course, can mean more than an error of management. It can frequently be moral failure. And here again, the response of integrity is specific. In referring to the Corinthians' response to his 'severe letter' in 2 Corinthians 7, Paul describes two possibilities: 'Godly sorrow brings repentance that leads to salvation and leaves no regret, but worldly sorrow brings death' (7:10).

In brief, *worldly sorrow* is the sorrow of being found out. We feel bad about the situation, but more because of its effect on us. It is self-centred sorrow. We feel angry and bitter, because we have been exposed. Our pride is wounded. The net result can be sourness, resentment, anger – 'death', Paul says.

The response of integrity is *godly sorrow*. The focus is not my wounded pride, but the God whom I have offended. It is characterized by godly grief, by an admission of wrongdoing and a genuine repentance. It opens the door to full restoration and so it leaves 'no regret' (7:10).

I have found this distinction a very helpful one. When I know I have failed, my initial response is often more aligned with worldly sorrow – self-defence, for example, or self-pity. But godly sorrow is the only thing which will help me find my way back.

The story of David teaches us much about recovering integrity. When the Lord appeared to Solomon, he said to him, 'As for you, if you walk before me in integrity of heart and uprightness, as David your father did ... ' (1 Kgs 9:4). David knew that God tested the heart and was 'pleased with integrity' (1 Chr. 29:17) – and he knew what it was to be exposed to the dangers and temptations of leadership.

Once he had risen to be king, he became careless. We know the story of his drift away from 'integrity of heart and uprightness'. He became indifferent to his military responsibilities in wartime, was tempted by the beauty of another man's wife, committed adultery and then tried to cover it up. The end result of his deception was the murder of his chief of staff. Yet God's purpose was to confront David with his sin and by his grace to restore him. David's response of godly sorrow was one of severe grief and deep repentance. It changed his life. We catch a glimpse of godly sorrow in one of his songs:

Create in me a pure heart, O God,
    and renew a steadfast spirit within me.
Do not cast me from your presence
    or take your Holy Spirit from me.
Restore to me to the joy of your salvation
    and grant me a willing spirit, to sustain me.
Then I will teach transgressors your ways,
    and sinners will turn back to you.
(Ps. 51:10–12)

It is a song taken on the lips of God's people throughout the centuries, for we know how much we need God's restoring grace. 'If we claim to be without sin, we deceive ourselves and the truth is not in us. If we confess our sins, he is faithful and just and will forgive us our sins and purify us from all unrighteousness' (1 John 1:8–9). And it is true. It is true! 'Therefore, since through God's mercy we have this ministry, we do not lose heart' (2 Cor. 4:1).

One final word of encouragement. There is another name in Paul's list at the end of 2 Timothy 4. 'Get Mark', Paul says, 'and bring him with you, because he is helpful to me in my ministry' (v. 11). This is a small but significant comment on restored integrity. Mark had been a real disappointment to Paul. He had been selected to go with Paul and Barnabas on the first missionary journey, but pretty soon Mark had jumped ship and abandoned the team. It was a tough trip and Mark obviously felt he was not up to it. He went home. So when it came to the preparations for the second missionary journey, Paul had already made up his mind about Mark. No thanks! He did not want to take him.

So there was a sharp disagreement between Paul and Barnabas, and we read about it in Acts 15:37–40. Barnabas was determined to take Mark, Paul disagreed, and so they parted company. Barnabas took Mark and Paul took Silas – and by God's grace it turned out that there were now two very fruitful missionary teams. Some twelve years later, Paul wrote to the Colossians and mentioned Mark, so he was obviously back in action with him (Col. 4:10–11). And it is clear that Mark was faithfully working with Peter too (1 Pet. 5:13). Maybe it was about twenty years after his original failure that Paul wrote these words in 2 Timothy: don't forget to bring Mark, it would be great to have his help. Mark is now fully restored.

Paul calls him 'useful', and this word is used only three times in the New Testament: here in 2 Timothy 4:11, earlier in 2:21 to describe useful utensils, and in a word play in Philemon 11 on the name of Onesimus (which means 'profitable'). So 'two useless people, both runaways who deserted their jobs, have become "useful" through the operation of God's grace in their lives'.[8] Even as an old man, Paul was big enough to change his mind, not to write Mark off but to give him a fresh chance to serve the Lord and to be part of the team. By God's grace, whatever the nature of our failure, there is a way back.

- 'My grace is sufficient for you, for my power is made perfect in weakness.' (2 Cor. 12:9)
- 'Therefore, since we have a great high priest who has gone through the heavens, Jesus the Son of God, let us hold firmly to the faith we profess. For we do not have a high priest who is unable to sympathize with our weaknesses, but we have one who has been tempted in every way, just as we are – yet was without sin. Let us then approach the throne of grace with confidence, so that we may receive mercy and find grace to help us in our time of need.' (Heb. 4:14–16)
- 'To him who is able to keep you from falling and to present you before his glorious presence without fault and with great joy – to the only God our Saviour be glory, majesty, power and authority, through Jesus Christ our Lord, before all ages, now and for evermore! Amen.' (Jude 24–25)

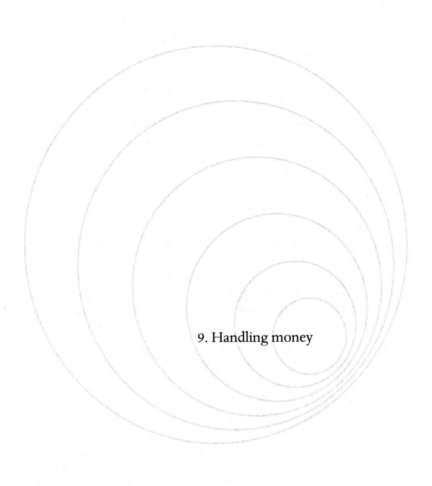

9. Handling money

When he was asked about his income, Joe Lewis once quipped, 'It doesn't matter whether you're rich or poor, as long as you've got money.' That is how many of us feel about the subject. We all have to live, we all have to make ends meet. So surely the matter of money is fairly neutral?

In fact, the issue of our use of money is right at the heart of our Christian discipleship. Paul devotes two full chapters to the subject in 2 Corinthians, because a range of other significant themes are attached to the matter of giving. They include our understanding of the gospel, the implications of fellowship, fundamental motivations in Christian living and discipleship, and even the nature of Christian worship. Far from being irrelevant to Christian leadership, money can be a critical issue where integrity is tested. How money is raised, how it is administered and how it is used all represent challenges for those charged with the leadership of a church or organization. As with each of the themes we are addressing, God is watching: Paul makes the point that, in the management of money, his representatives are being watched not only by the churches but by God himself (8:20–21).

Paul was concerned to encourage the Corinthians to make a contribution to an urgent project – an offering for the special needs of the believers in Jerusalem, who were under considerable financial pressure. As converted Jews they faced the hostility of their families and neighbours, and probably many of them lost their employment as a result. Then it is likely that those in work had only menial jobs, hardly securing enough income to cover the needs of their families, let alone the wider Christian community in the city. On top of that we know that they were suffering from a famine, which added to the pressure.

So Paul was anxious that a collection be taken from around the region, not only to meet the needs of the Christians in Jerusalem, but also as an expression of solidarity between Jewish and Gentile believers. Such practical action would be a clear signal of the unity of believers from different cultural backgrounds. The two chapters contain a great deal of valuable teaching on the issue of Christian giving, but our purpose here is to highlight issues surrounding leadership and integrity. The approach employed by Paul, coupled with his teaching, have several significant things to say on this theme.

There are three introductory principles in 2 Corinthians 8 which demonstrate why handling money in the Christian community must be carried out with wise stewardship and scrupulous care.

First, Christian giving is *spiritual*. This might come as a surprise to those of us used to talking about filthy lucre! But generous giving is the result of God's grace working in our lives. Notice how frequently Paul makes reference to this: 'the grace that God has given the Macedonian churches' (8:1); 'this act of grace' (8:6); 'the grace of giving' (8:7); 'the grace of our Lord Jesus Christ' (8:9); 'God is able to make all grace abound to you' (9:8); 'because of the surpassing grace God has given you' (9:14).

It is made more explicit when Paul explains that the Macedonian response was the result of giving themselves 'first to the Lord' (8:5). Their financial generosity arose from their wholehearted commitment to the lordship of Christ. Everything was surrendered to him. Here is an important principle. True Christian giving is triangular: we give first to the Lord, then for something or someone. This immediately calls for integrity. To see giving in this way removes any sense of manipulation on the part of the giver ('now I have some influence over this project'), and also removes any sense of embarrassment or indebtedness on the part of the receiver. We are giving to God, as part of the total stewardship and worship of our lives.

Second, Christian giving is *sacrificial*. It must have been God's grace at work, because the Macedonian Christians gave when they could ill afford to do so. They too were under pressure of persecution, and Paul says they suffered from 'extreme poverty' (8:2). Yet despite these constraints, their sacrificial giving was characterized by two qualities. It was generous. Paul calls it 'rich generosity' (8:2), and in chapter 9 he reminds the Corinthians that this is the kind of giving God looks for. These Christians gave well beyond their means (8:3). It was also willing (8:3; 9:7). There was no need for Paul to urge them to give – indeed, he seems to have been reluctant to make any appeal to them because of their poverty (8:3–4), and the Macedonians pleaded with him to be allowed to make their contribution. Paul repeats this theme in chapter 9: 'Each man should give what he has decided in his heart to give, not reluctantly or under compulsion, for God loves a cheerful giver' (9:7).

So it should be for all Christians. Not meanness, not careful calculation, not a qualified use of our time or money or resources, but everything made available for God's purposes. It has been a moving and humbling experience for my family as, over the years of our Christian service, we have been supported in prayer and finance by many friends, some of whom are elderly widows with limited financial resources. They have faithfully pledged a small monthly gift to the organizations with which we have been working, and we know that this has been sacrificial giving. It provokes within us a deep sense of gratitude and a strong concern that finances in our work must be well deployed.

Third, Christian giving *expresses solidarity*. The giving of the Macedonians was also motivated by a concern for the well-being of other Christians, a desire to have 'the privilege of sharing in this service to the saints' (8:4). Their sense of solidarity with their fellow believers in the body of Christ provoked them to give to the needs of others. Such unselfishness is a mark of true fellowship.

If these three basic principles are at the front of our minds as we handle money in Christian community, it will save us from many potential errors or temptations. We will realize that we are responsible for the wise stewardship of the Lord's resources, not our own; that we are responsible for limited resources, given sacrificially by fellow believers; and that money, used prayerfully, can be the means to strengthen Christian fellowship in significant ways.

On this foundation we should notice the practical care which Paul took in the administration of the project. How he manages money is critical. It is a fundamental test of integrity and consistency. So he declares, 'We want to avoid any criticism of the way we administer this liberal gift. For we are taking pains to do what is right, not only in the eyes of the Lord but also in the eyes of men' (8:20). The seriousness with which Paul viewed the collection is expressed not only in his appeal to the Corinthians to complete the task and send in their generous contribution, but also by his responsible management of the entire operation. There are four key lessons.

Working together

Paul refers to several of his fellow workers who were partners with him in this ministry. Titus was a great supporter of the project (8:16–17). He was ready to travel to Corinth and was enthusiastic about receiving their money. He was accompanied by a well-known brother – so well known that Paul need not name him, but there are some suggestions that it might have been Luke.[1] Significantly, Paul identifies him in relation to his faithful service to the gospel (8:18). There was a further partner, referred to in verse 22, also marked out as 'zealous'.

Paul is demonstrating here that the collection of the offering was committed to faithful, proven servants of the churches, men who were committed to the gospel and clearly trusted. In Acts 6, when the church needed to appoint people who were to relieve the apostles of time-consuming practical tasks, they chose men 'full of the Spirit'. The point is that whatever the task within the Christian community, spiritual qualifications are needed. This is important in the area of financial management, whether counting the Sunday offering, or looking after the petty cash in the office, or administering the funds of a Christian organization. Paul's fellow workers were some of the best, and he could rely on their faithful ministry and enthusiastic participation, as men of integrity and trust.

In our churches or Christian organizations we must be careful to ensure that decisions with regard to money are not made by one person alone. We should ensure that information about finances is governed not by a culture of secrecy but by a culture of transparency. That is an essential part of leading with integrity today, and in many countries it will be countercultural. We should not minimize the pressures which those working in countries with very limited resources must face. The temptation to use funds, given for one purpose, for an entirely different purpose – because of financial pressure and cash flow difficulties – is very real indeed. The potential conflict of interest for many Christians is acute: they face distressing family needs, while at the same time handling substantial funds from outside the country for church buildings or projects. Those of us in comfortable situations in the West cannot easily empathize with these temptations. But whatever our circumstances, we must ask for God's grace to act honestly.

Careful administration

Such use of trusted fellow workers was part of a policy of wise management. Paul spent considerable effort in ensuring not only that things were done properly, but that they were seen to be done properly (8:21). First, as we have seen, fellow workers were essential if Paul was to avoid any potential criticism (8:20). It was clearly a substantial offering, and so Paul needed fellow travellers to ensure adequate protection.

Working as a team is important in every aspect of church life, because of the special benefits of shared gifts, mutual support and encouragement. But a further vital benefit is accountability. This is particularly important in the area of financial administration.

Second, as we have seen, such fellow workers need to be trusted colleagues with the right spiritual and practical qualities for the job. It is important to be honest here: the temptation to misuse funds probably comes a close second to sexual temptation, not only amongst leaders but amongst all believers, although leaders sometimes face more opportunities to be tempted than the rest of us. Since it can be a device of Satan to exploit potential weakness, it is always important in church affairs to ensure that there is careful administration similar to that which Paul employed. Even the most trustworthy treasurer needs others to work with him or her in counting money and signing cheques, so that we 'take pains to do what is right, not only in the eyes of the Lord but also in the eyes of men'. We are leading with God watching. So our handling of money must be transparent.

Creating ownership

This section also reinforces the theme of the early part of the chapter: the offering itself is an expression of Christian fellowship (8:4), but the way in which Paul administered the collection also reflected the corporate solidarity of the churches. He refers to this when commenting on his fellow workers: 'the brother who is praised by all the churches ... was chosen by the churches to accompany us as we carry the offering' (8:18, 19). Clearly there was a sense of ownership of the project, with the churches involved in selecting the team of helpers. Similarly, he reinforces the sense of partnership when he refers to Titus as a 'fellow worker among you', and to the brothers as 'representatives of the churches' (8:23). This is not just the initiative of Paul or of Titus. This is a shared project of the churches, all of whom feel a sense of engagement in making it happen.

This was also part of Paul's appeal to the Corinthians. If his fellow workers are representatives of the churches, then it is important that the Corinthians respect them, welcoming them as they arrive to take up the offering, and demonstrating their love for their fellow believers in the practical commitment to give. This was part of their solidarity with others – 'so that the churches can see it', Paul urges them (8:24). This built trust and created partnership.

While there are some occasions when a degree of confidentiality is needed, particularly if the donor wishes that to be the case, in almost all other situations it is best for the handling of money to be completely open. I once served in an organization that decided to keep financial details of the allocation of funds within the team confidential between those team members, all of whom were trusted with the responsibility of deploying funds in different parts of the world. There were good reasons for this. If fellow workers heard about the sums of money being used in one region or another, jealousy or misunderstanding would be the result. But in fact the policy engendered a degree of suspicion. Why is this secret? Is there a hidden agenda on the part of the small financial team who have all the information? We wondered if it would have been better for the policy to have been one of complete transparency within the team, coupled with careful explanation and a commitment to building trust. The offering which Paul administered had to be seen to be managed carefully – and we too should 'take pains to do what is right, not only in the eyes of the Lord but also in the eyes of men'.

Honouring the Lord

To reinforce the fact that the offering is part of their worship, Paul refers several times to the importance of honouring the Lord. The administration of the offering by the team of fellow workers was 'to honour the Lord himself' (8:19). The careful procedures they adopted were to ensure that everything was done correctly 'in the eyes of the Lord' (8:21). And the faithful partners in taking up the offering were 'an honour to Christ' (8:23).

Nothing was done in a haphazard or slapdash way; no opportunity was given for criticism; nothing was allowed to dishonour the name of Christ. This should be true of every aspect of our work. Our purpose is not to build our own organization or reputation, or attract attention to our own skills and successes, but to honour Christ. That is why the church is here.

If we handle money in this way, there will be a productive result. There is a ripple effect from generous giving.

First, *the giver will be enriched*. Paul explains in chapter 9 that the Corinthians will be 'made rich in every way so that you can be generous on every occasion' (v. 11). God's provision for them will mean that they will be able to be still more generous, for that is the way God works. He provides more so that we can give more.

Second, *the recipient benefits*. Their giving supplies 'the needs of God's people' (9:12). The service of giving is an act of worship, and clearly the initial reason for the collection was to meet the needs of hard-pressed Christians in Jerusalem. They in turn will respond with thanksgiving as God meets their needs.

Third, *the Christian community benefits*. When Christians give sacrificially and generously, it reflects the fact that they have experienced the grace of the gospel and understood the dynamics of Christian fellowship. Paul explains that the convincing proof of their acceptance of the gospel was their practical obedience: 'men will praise God for the obedience that accompanies your confession of the gospel of Christ' (9:13). The evidence was their practical commitment to giving. Then in the same verse he refers to their 'generosity in sharing with them and with everyone else' (9:13). Giving has to do with our commitment to the gospel of God and the people of God. Good stewardship, a generous spirit and a commitment to live our lives for others rather than for ourselves are an inevitable consequence of how the Christian gospel impacts our lives.

Fourth, *God is praised*. This result is the most significant of all, and Paul refers to it repeatedly. Their generosity 'will result in thanksgiving to God' (9:11), 'is also overflowing in many expressions of thanks to God' (9:12), and it will provoke men to 'praise God' (9:13). The way Christians give and receive will bring glory to God himself. The immediate goal of the collection was to alleviate the needs of hard-pressed Christians, but the ultimate goal was to encourage greater honour and praise to God. That is how we should see our giving in our churches, and the giving of our lives in generous service to others. That is always our ultimate goal – God's glory.

Yet alongside Paul's teaching on the profound theological foundations for our wise use of money, we can see Christian integrity displayed at every point in his practical management of the project.

We should not underestimate the subtle temptations facing those of us who control budgets, count offerings, or handle expenses. At every point integrity demands a trustworthy team, transparent administration, genuine partnership and an awareness that we serve under the watchful eye of the Lord himself.

Section C – Over to you . . .

- In what ways are you tempted to exercise authority inappropriately, and how do you measure up compared to the meekness and gentleness of Christ?
- Is there somebody in your network of relationships to whom you must express forgiveness more directly?
- None of us can live a life of integrity without also feeling the disappointment of failure. If you are particularly conscious of this, what are the steps you can take to recover integrity?
- I have just received an email from someone who stole money at a Christian conference fifteen years ago and now wishes to put the matter right. Are there areas of inconsistency in your handling of money – official or unofficial, large or small – which might need to be addressed as a matter of integrity?
- Within the Christian community, where would you say the balance lies between confidentiality and transparency? What are the circumstances in which confidentiality must be maintained, and what are the benefits of encouraging transparency at every appropriate opportunity?

D. Leadership and its challenges

10. Weakness and power

A short while ago I met a Latvian pastor by the name of Josef Bondarenko. We spoke together at the Keston Institute in Oxford, where he gave a lecture on church life in the Baltic States. I was keen to meet him because, thirty years ago, I had his photograph on the wall of my student bedsit. He was a pastor serving in what was then the Soviet Union, and was one of many people who had been imprisoned for his faith. Hence his photo – along with about thirty others – placed on my wall as a daily reminder to pray for the church under pressure. In fact, he suffered three periods of imprisonment for proclaiming the Christian message, and many years in exile in Siberian work camps. In his lecture to us in Oxford some years after the collapse of the Soviet empire, he spoke movingly of the fact that his family still suffered the results of that period of hardship and exile, but shared his resolve to persevere in their Christian calling.

Of course, this is one example of what continues to happen the world over. It has been estimated that in 1999, 164,000 Christians died for their faith. At present some 200 million evangelicals in thirty-five countries are suffering direct and hostile persecution. It is a reminder that the kind of pressure Josef Bondarenko faced is still exerted on thousands of Christians today.

Christian service is often very sacrificial, and always costly. I cannot help contrasting this with the attitudes we sometimes encounter today – that Christian ministry is something which I can exercise so that I can be fulfilled as a person, so that I can discover my gift or find my place in the church. Of course, there is a positive aspect to today's interest in discovering our ministry and developing our gifts. It asserts that every Christian is needed, every Christian is called to serve God, and we need to help one another to discover that ministry and exercise it faithfully. Yet the fact of the matter is that all true Christian ministry is costly. Christianity is not romantic, it is not soft. Christian ministry takes its toll, and in 2 Corinthians Paul is completely realistic about that. Few biblical books make the point more clearly than his testimony in this letter.

As we reflect on the theme of integrity in leadership, I wonder how we view the issue of weakness. Would it not be true that the qualities we look for in Christian leaders are surprisingly similar to those we would expect in a company chief executive? Would there be many differences between the leadership profile we draw up for a Christian organization and one prepared for a secular one? After all, we expect strength. Leaders are people who cope. They are bold, assertive, powerful. They are in control. The literature on leadership a few years ago used 'power language'. Executives carry a power briefcase and they wear a power suit. They clinch deals at power breakfasts. They admit to no weakness, but exude confidence with every commanding step they take.

Halfway through the election campaign in the UK in 2005, Charles Kennedy, then leader of the Liberal Democrats, was mocked because, in a morning televised interview, he was confused over the issue of tax policy. Kennedy defended himself by explaining that he was suffering from sleep deprivation following the birth of his first child. A reporter on Sky TV commented that it showed him to be more human than the other party leaders – and 'that's not what we are looking for in a leader'. A leader . . . human? Not quite what we want.

As we have seen, Paul confronted similar attitudes and expectations in his day. Indeed, it was precisely because he failed to match up to their image of power and celebrity that he was criticized so aggressively. But the significant feature of 2 Corinthians is this: Paul explains that at the heart of the Christian message, and therefore at the heart of all Christian ministry, lies a painful paradox. It is a paradox which modern secular people, with their passion for power and prestige, regard as foolishness. But for Christians it is the only thing that makes sense of the gospel and of our Christian service. We find it in 2 Corinthians 12:9, 'My grace is sufficient for you, for my power is made perfect in weakness.'

This word from the Lord represented an important breakthrough for Paul. He came to understand his weakness in relation to the gospel message which he preached. What was the gospel, after all? It was God at work through the weakness of the crucified Jesus, God's power displayed in the apparent weakness and foolishness of the cross. So it was no surprise that the gospel should reach the Gentiles through the weakness of the apostle. What Paul came to understand was that, in carrying out God's work, human resources have their limits. We look at the size and urgency of the task and compare that with the resources at our disposal; we look at the opposition that we encounter and the god of this world who lies behind it; and we can become weighed down not only by the burden of human need all around us, but with our own feelings of inadequacy, doubt or frailty.

To do this is not to be defeatist. When Paul reflected on his weakness he was being realistic. He had been pushed to the limits of his endurance, as he explains in the catalogue of sufferings in 2 Corinthians 11. His missionary work was quite literally killing him. And it was not only the opposition which he experienced from those who contested the spread of the gospel; not only the physical hardships of sleepless nights and multiple beatings. One of the most painful experiences, as we have seen, was the opposition which was gathering momentum within the church at Corinth. After all Paul had done to bring them the gospel and share his life with them, others were casting doubt on his ministry and motives as an apostle. But Paul had come to understand that it was precisely at this point that God's power was displayed. He had understood his weakness in relation to the theology of the cross. His struggles were a mark of true discipleship, the result of fellowship with Christ and, indeed, the essential prerequisite for effective Christian ministry.

It is important to stress that such weakness does not refer to some pale brand of the Christian faith. It is not flabby, wet, indecisive Christianity. As Paul explains earlier in his letter, 'Therefore, since we have such a hope, we are very bold' (3:12). He was courageous, outspoken and showed almost no fear as he took on the challenge of mission in the first century. Rather, Paul is describing his own feelings of frailty and powerlessness, his own emotional vulnerability, his feelings of anxiety and maybe even depression, the pain of opposition and persecution, all of which he endured as a servant of the suffering Master for whom he was an ambassador. He had come to see that it was through such weakness that God's power would be displayed. And so he could boast, 'when I am weak, then I am strong' (12:10). As a child I was encouraged by my father, who used a simple but memorable illustration: Christians are like tea – their real strength is drawn only when they get into hot water.

So we turn to the second part of 2 Corinthians 4 to explore how Paul was able to live with integrity in the midst of the pressures of Christian service.

Weakness is the occasion for God's power
We have already explored the gospel priorities which shape our ministry through our examination of 2 Corinthians 4:1–6. We are to

proclaim Christ clearly and faithfully, for God has given us 'the light of the knowledge of the glory of God in the face of Jesus Christ' (4:6). But as Paul writes about the power and the glory of the gospel, he is reminded by contrast of his own frailty and weakness. 'But we have this treasure in jars of clay' (4:7).

This is one of Paul's familiar metaphors and it suggests a number of images. One is of a cheap pottery lamp. It carries the light, and the more cracks it contains, the more the light will shine through. The second possibility is a reference to the triumphal procession of an army, about which he spoke in 2 Corinthians 2:14. Perhaps the jars of clay are the pots in which, after victory at war, valuable treasure is displayed. So there would be a stark contrast between the container and the treasure. These were ordinary clay jars, and even today you find them used in the Middle East despite the availability of plastic. They are used for all sorts of purposes, and they are easily broken.

Paul's point is to highlight the contrast, to emphasize the paradox. On the one hand, the majesty and the power of the message; on the other, the weak, buffeted, fragile messenger. He was painfully aware of all the limitations placed on him by the frailty of his human nature. The reason for this is very important: 'to show that this all-surpassing power is from God and not from us' (4:7). Paul himself was a good example of this principle. Apparently, in terms of his physical appearance he was hardly Arnold Schwarzenegger. His physical frame might not have been impressive, his speech might not have been up to much, and he probably had eye trouble. Good, he says. For when people are converted everyone will know it is down to the power of the gospel. He said much the same in his first letter: 'that your faith might not rest on men's wisdom, but on God's power' (1 Cor. 2:5).

As we have seen, this is exactly the case with the gospel itself, as Paul explains in 1 Corinthians 1:20–25. 'The foolishness of God is wiser than man's wisdom, and the weakness of God is stronger than man's strength.' The same paradox is expressed in the Corinthian congregation too. God chose the foolish, the weak, the low and the despised – and thereby confounded the strong. Why did he do that? 'So that no-one may boast before him' (1 Cor. 1:29).

In an excellent book on leadership, based on expositions of 1 Corinthians 1 – 4, John Stott highlights the paradox expressed in these verses. 'For God chose a weak instrument (Paul), to bring a weak message (the cross) to weak people (the Corinthian working class). But through this triple weakness the power of God was – and still is – displayed.'[1]

To reinforce the point, in 2 Corinthians 4 Paul gives a series of comparisons to demonstrate the weakness he regularly felt in his ministry and the simultaneous experience of God's power. In verses 8 and 9 he presents a series of contrasts. It is a clever piece of writing, since each of the pairs contains a play on words. I once saw an Italian ice cream van bearing the slogan 'Luigi's ice cream – often licked, but never beaten'. This captures both the sentiment and the style of Paul's writing in this section.

- The first pair is possibly an illustration from boxing, with the fighter giving his opponent very little room for manoeuvre, but unable to drive him into the corner: 'hard pressed ... but not crushed', or 'hemmed in but not hamstrung'.
- The second pair has a similar play on words, paraphrased by James Denny: 'put to it, but not utterly put out'.
- The third pair describes Paul feeling pursued like a hunted man: you might say, 'hunted by men but never abandoned by God'.
- The fourth pair demonstrates that, even when hunted down, he is never completely defeated: 'struck down, but not destroyed', or 'often felled, never finished'. Or, as J. B. Phillips paraphrases, 'they can knock me down but they cannot knock me out'.

Paul is expressing here what Christians through the centuries have experienced. It is the experience of most Christian leaders – of being stretched almost to the limit in our service for God, of feeling the exhaustion and the disappointments, the setbacks and the pressures. Anyone who throws themselves into the work of God will feel this. But the experience of all God's people is this: that the end of our resources is not the end of God's. It is at moments of pressure and weakness – sometimes at very extreme moments – that we are in the best position to prove God's grace and power. The Dutch Christian Betsie ten Boom is recorded as speaking bravely in the Ravensbrück concentration camp during World War II. 'We must tell them that there is no pit so deep, that God is not deeper still.' This is the essence of what Paul is describing. However desperate the circumstances, the Christian believer can know God's strengthening presence and empowering grace.

These verses are a great challenge and encouragement for us, applicable in every area of Christian service. But they are especially worth reflecting on in a day of evangelical triumphalism. Missiologist David Smith asks penetrating questions about the church's task in a globalized context. He comments, for example, on the literature of mission organizations which breathes a 'can do' spirit based on the recognition of the power available through the gifts of modern technology. He comments, 'A consultation to discuss the completion of the Great Commission . . . is described in language which betrays a fascination with the power of technology.' The meeting took place in a special 'Global Strategy Room' that was 'like being on the navigation bridge of the Enterprise . . .' Amid 140 'Action Points' and 168 'AD2000 Global Goals', the group meeting in this *Star Trek* environment proposed to 'initiate co-operation between 42 million computers owned by Christians . . . create a worldwide electronic Great Commission network . . . maintain a computerised calendar of all related events past and future'.[2]

All of us would affirm the importance of prayerful strategic planning and global partnership. But those of us who come from dominant and powerful cultures, as David Smith points out, must now ask how we should do mission from such a position – and 2 Corinthians shows us that the principles which should govern our ministry strategies should be filtered through the mesh of the gospel priorities of the weakness of the crucified Jesus. Integrity in Christian service demands this.

I have often reflected on how Isaiah described the low-profile ministry of the Servant in Isaiah 42. If we might make a brief diversion, it is worth reflecting on the characteristics of the Servant's ministry as Isaiah portrays it.

Dependence: 'Here is my servant, whom I uphold.' (Isa. 42:1)
Jesus voluntarily abandoned everything on which we might have relied. Born in a manger, brought up in a despised province and in a third-rate town, equipped with no human advantages of wealth or education, no influential power base and no impressive sponsors, he was the Servant: obedient to and dependent upon his Father. 'My servant, whom I uphold.'

Quietness: 'He will not shout or cry out, or raise his voice in the streets.' (Isa. 42:2)

The cumulative emphasis describes a ministry which is quiet and unassuming. It is not self-advertising, nor interested in power or prestige. Jesus' strategy of mission was often low key, and usually with the small and apparently insignificant people.

Gentleness: 'A bruised reed he will not break, and a smouldering wick he will not snuff out.' (Isa. 42:3)

Both of the pictures in this verse are images of fragility. To the Servant, nothing is useless. However it came to be crushed, however close to extinction, it can be restored. In his mission to the needy, the Servant identified with the weaknesses of those he came to save.[3]

In a media-conscious age, churches and Christian organizations inevitably face the temptation to strengthen their marketing and PR budgets. Christian leaders are under pressure to portray an image of strength and influence. But the ministry of the Servant in Isaiah, the Master in Galilee and the apostle in Corinth all imply there is another way. God's power is seen in weakness.

Weakness is the consequence of being united to Christ

Why is it that all Christians must walk this pathway? Why is the experience of weakness inevitable? From 4:10 onwards Paul sums up the theme and explains the significance of his experience in relation to the gospel itself. Paul shows that his experience is a reflection of the dying life of Jesus and the renewing power of God that raised Jesus from death. Look at the sequence of verses:

- 'We always carry around in our body the death of Jesus.' (v. 10)
- 'We . . . are always being given over to death for Jesus' sake.' (v. 11)
- 'The one who raised the Lord Jesus . . . will also raise us with Jesus.' (v. 14)

Paul is saying that he is sharing his Master's earthly experience. Four times in verses 10 and 11 he refers to 'Jesus' the man. And the word he uses in verse 10 could be translated 'the dying of Jesus' – it is the process of dying, of putting to death, rather than the final condition of death. He always parades the dying of Jesus. When we read Paul's catalogues of suffering we can understand this. At times he probably looked just like someone in the process of dying, someone being crucified. He expresses this in graphic terms elsewhere in his writing:

- 'the sufferings of Christ flow over into our lives' (2 Cor. 1:5);
- 'if indeed we share in his sufferings' (Rom. 8:17);
- 'I bear on my body the marks of Jesus' (Gal. 6:17).

So if you are a Christian, united to Christ, there is no avoiding this, and we should suspect all models of the Christian life or Christian spirituality which try to remove such weakness. We are disciples of the crucified Jesus. We live in union with him. But if we are united with Jesus in his death, we are also united in his resurrection. We share with Jesus the suffering and the glory, since our life is bound up with his.

- '[We are] given over to death ... so that his life may be revealed in our mortal body.' (4:11)
- 'The one who raised the Lord Jesus from the dead will also raise us with Jesus.' (4:14)

The resurrection is not confined to a future life, but is already a part of our experience. So now the life of Jesus is manifest in our body:

- 'dying, and yet we live on' (6:9);
- 'For to be sure, he was crucified in weakness, yet he lives by God's power. Likewise, we are weak in him, yet by God's power we will live with him to serve you.' (13:4)

This transforms our perspective on the many challenges associated with our Christian service. We are not immune from pressures, for they are an inevitable consequence of our association with Jesus. God's purpose is not to bypass weaknesses and difficulties, but to transform them.

I remember my first experience of sailing. I joined a crew circum-navigating the island of Mull off the coast of Scotland. The weather was quite severe and the boat was being blown over to what seemed like a 45 degree angle. That was one occasion when having one leg shorter than the other – as I do – was a positive advantage. Everyone else was falling over while I remained upright! We used the rather uncomfortable manoeuvre of 'beating', facing the wind and tacking in one direction and then another. It was painfully slow, but we were using the winds which were against us in order to make progress forward. That seems to me to be a realistic model of Christian discipleship. When we face difficulties, God will not beam us up to heaven, but he will transform those circumstances in ways which will fulfil his purpose. Evil has lost the initiative. God will take those very winds which are against us and use them to help us make progress forward.

Weakness is productive

Far from being a handicap, weakness produces a range of positive outcomes which Paul outlines in the closing verses of 2 Corinthians 4. The sense of paradox continues, as he shows that the more battered he is, the better it will be for the cause of Christian mission. There are three productive results.

It produces dependence

On the basis of his trust in Jesus, Paul could continue his ministry of preaching the gospel. Even if it was a costly experience in terms of personal suffering, he could not keep quiet. In 4:13 he quotes from Psalm 116:10, which records how the psalmist had been delivered from a near-death experience and its profound emotional impact. It was perhaps a very similar experience to that which Paul describes in 2 Corinthians 1. God had delivered the psalmist, and God had delivered Paul. So now he was determined not to give up – 'we do not lose heart' (4:16) – but to continue with the same spirit of faith as the psalmist. 'I believed; therefore I have spoken.'

In chapter 1 Paul demonstrates how this works. Such was the pressure of his suffering that he almost despaired of life – but the end result was a determined confidence in God, a dependence that he would never otherwise have exercised. 'But this happened that we might not rely on ourselves but on God, who raises the dead' (1:9). So it will be for us. Pressures will provoke a strengthening of our faith. They result in what Jim Packer calls 'adult godliness'.

It benefits others

- 'So then, death is at work in us, but life is at work in you.' (4:12)
- 'All this is for your benefit.' (4:15)

In chapter 4 we suggested that Christian service had a basic orientation. Leaders do not say 'here I am', but 'there you are'. Their work is for the benefit of others, 'for your sake'. Now in 2 Corinthians 4 Paul states this even more starkly, as he concludes his testimony to the weaknesses he has experienced. 'Death is at work in us, but life is at work in you.' It is possible that there is some irony here, a deliberate teasing of the Corinthians, as Tom Wright suggests, 'that they think they must only have the life of Jesus, while all he has is the death of Jesus'. Is he challenging them to think more carefully about what it means to identify with Jesus' death?[4]

We can also understand it with reference to chapter 1: 'If we are distressed, it is for your comfort and salvation' (1:6). His experience of dying actually serves to bring life and salvation to the Corinthians. They are the beneficiaries of all that Paul went through. So in 4:15, the 'all this' – including his suffering and his dying – is for their benefit.

That is an uncomfortable aspect our calling as Christian leaders: to sacrifice ourselves for the benefit of those whom we serve. I am not sure it is a common expectation of leaders. Surely we have reached a position where others make the sacrifices? Not so. The connection is in the text, to which we referred when describing our call to serve others in chapter 4. It was 'for your benefit', for the Corinthians' sake (4:15), because it was 'for Jesus' sake' (4:5).

The 48 Laws of Power is marketed as 'the definitive guide to modern manipulation'. Found in the business section of airport bookshops, Robert Greene's book might be tongue in cheek, but it gets close to the truth in terms of contemporary attitudes. It stands at the opposite pole from 2 Corinthians. You get the flavour from some of the 'laws of power' which he lists.

Law 2: Never put too much trust in friends, learn how to use enemies.
Law 3: Conceal your intentions.
Law 6: Court attention at all costs.

Law 7: Get others to do the work for you, but always take the credit.

Law 20: Do not commit to anyone.

Law 42: Strike the shepherd and the sheep will scatter.

'The key to power', Greene suggests, 'is the ability to judge who is best able to further your interests in all situations.'[5] By contrast, shall we pause and reflect on some keys to effective leadership from Paul?

- 'If we are distressed, it is for your comfort and salvation.' (2 Cor. 1:6)
- 'Death is at work in us, but life is at work in you.' (2 Cor. 4:12)
- 'All this is for your benefit.' (2 Cor. 4:15)
- 'I will very gladly spend for you everything I have and expend myself as well.' (2 Cor. 12:15)
- 'Even if I am being poured out like a drink offering on the sacrifice and service coming from your faith, I am glad and rejoice with all of you.' (Phil. 2:17)
- 'I rejoice in what was suffered for you, and I fill up in my flesh what is still lacking in regard to Christ's afflictions, for the sake of his body, which is the church. I have become its servant by the commission God gave me.' (Col. 1:24–25)
- 'We loved you so much that we were delighted to share with you not only the gospel of God but our lives as well.' (1 Thess. 2:8)
- 'I endure everything for the sake of the elect, that they too may obtain the salvation which is in Christ Jesus, with eternal glory.' (2 Tim. 2:10)

It will not sell in airport bookshops, but it is the gracious law of Christian service which arises from the gospel of Jesus Christ. Weakness in our ministry will be for the eternal benefit of those whom we serve.

It results in God's glory

All this is for your benefit, so that the grace that is reaching more and more people may cause thanksgiving to overflow to the glory of God. (2 Cor. 4:15)

Here is Paul's third positive conclusion. All the trials which he presently endures are put into perspective by the fact that not only are they for the benefit of the Corinthians, but, more importantly, they are for the glory of God. Being a minister of the gospel was a tough job. It cost Paul all he had. He was not in it for personal gain, however, but for the glory of the God who called him to service. It resulted ultimately in the only thing that really matters – God's glory.

The sequence in verse 15 is a lovely description of the impact of the gospel:

- the gospel reaches more and more people;
- the result is more and more thanksgiving;
- the thanksgiving overflows into a greater declaration of God's glory.

We can put up with a great deal if we know what the end result will be. Here Paul expresses it in a profoundly moving way. What is the result of all of the discouragement, the pressure, the criticism, the personal cost? It is a sequence of eternal realities: God's grace impacting more lives, God's people rejoicing in his victories, God's glory being the eventual goal of all we have passed through.

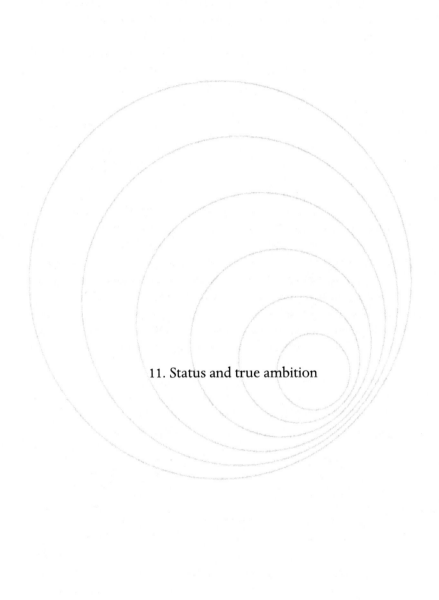

11. Status and true ambition

The devil was once crossing the Libyan desert, and he came upon
a spot where a number of small fiends were tormenting a holy
hermit. The sainted man easily shook off their evil suggestions.
The devil watched their failure, and he stepped forward to give
them a lesson. 'What you do is too crude,' he said. 'Permit me
for one moment.' With that he whispered to the holy man,
'Your brother has just been made Bishop of Alexandria.' A scowl
of malignant jealousy at once clouded the serene face of the hermit.
'That', said the devil to his imps, 'is the sort of thing which I should
recommend.'[1]

Few of us are immune from 'status anxiety', as it is called these days.
Alain de Botton defines it in this way: 'it is a worry so pernicious as to
be capable of ruining extended stretches of our lives, that we are in
danger of failing to conform to the ideals of success laid down by our
society, and that we may as a result be stripped of dignity and respect;
a worry that we are currently occupying too modest a rung or about
to fall to a lower one'. He says you can spot status anxiety in people in
a variety of ways, including 'an over-extended pause after news of
another's achievement'.[2]

Christian leaders are not immune from this. We are often anxious
about how we measure up. Concerns about status bubble up
surprisingly frequently. Sometimes we encounter it when people
assert that a certain task is beneath them. I once worked with someone
who kept on appealing 'but it's not in my job description'. Sometimes it has to do with an insistence that 'rank' is properly observed. I
guess it is less common amongst the younger generation, but I know
someone who insists that their proper designation of 'Reverend'
always be used in public. Jo Owen, one of the founders of the Teach
First initiative (which takes graduates and places them in inner-
city primary schools for two years before they enter the corporate
sector), comments on leadership styles in his book *How to Lead*. He
suggests that you can spot one category, the 'aristocrat', in this way.
'Try asking someone what they do. If they reply, "I am a partner/
vice-president/senior manager/director at . . . ", they are not telling
you what they do. They are telling you about their title and position.
This is what is important to them. Work and achievement are
unfortunate, grubby barriers they have to jump on the way to title

and status.'[3] But it is still more subtle. Sometimes we judge status by the secular standards of activism and achievement.

In a recent paper from the Institute for Social and Economic Research, the suggestion was made that being busy is 'the new badge of honour'. Working long hours and staying late at the office is becoming a status symbol. This can be a subtle temptation to Christian workers too. Sometimes our drivenness and activism are the result not of the demands of our work, but of the expectation of others. Eugene Peterson once wrote an essay entitled 'The Unbusy Pastor', in which he says that if you are visiting a doctor's surgery and find that no one is waiting to see him, and you look through the doorway to see him reading a book, you naturally begin to wonder if he is any good. Surely a good doctor will be frantically busy, with people lined up to see him. Sometimes our drivenness is the result of our own desire to be seen as significant. (Peterson even goes so far as to suggest that 'the adjective *busy* set as a modifier to *pastor* should sound to our ears like *adulterous* to characterize a wife or *embezzling* to describe a banker. It is an outrageous scandal, a blasphemous affront.' If only!)[4]

Then we also face the temptation to nudge aside service and sacrifice and use the language of success. Comparisons between churches can often be measured by numbers, by the standard of performance, by income, or by reputation. Christian leaders can be measured by career path, speaking skills, influence in the evangelical world, or the size of the church. Tony Campolo once suggested that the tendency for growing churches to start new building programmes arises from the fact that leaders might suffer from an 'edifice complex' – the need 'to erect a monument to their successful leadership'. Few of us are immune from the temptations of success and status.

The lessons from Paul's defence to the Corinthians are very timely. We sense something of the discomfort he obviously feels. This is not simply the discomfort associated with the criticisms he is encountering, but the discomfort of having to write about himself, of 'boasting about' or 'commending' himself. But the Corinthians have forced him into it and, for the rest of the letter from chapter 10 onwards, he will have to 'boast' in order to expose the empty rhetoric of the teachers who are capturing the minds and hearts of the believers for whom he cares so much.

It goes against the grain, as we shall see, but Paul skilfully turns the tables on those for whom such boasting is an integral part of their egocentric lives. The lessons of the final part of 2 Corinthians 10 are a reminder of what true ambition looks like for the servant of the Lord.

The folly of self-commendation

First, Paul mocks his critics in Corinth by showing how foolish they are to commend themselves. In fact, there is a fair amount of sarcasm here, as J. B. Phillips's paraphrase demonstrates: 'Of course, we shouldn't dare to include ourselves in the same class as those who write their own testimonials. We shouldn't even dare to compare ourselves with them' (10:12).

They doubtless arrived in Corinth carrying special letters of commendation. I was brought up within a Christian tradition where such letters were commonplace. If our family was visiting another church while we were on holiday, it would not be unusual for my father to carry a letter from our home church, introducing us to the new congregation. Although sometimes referred to in our family as a letter of condemnation rather than commendation, it performed a valuable function. It was a thoughtful expression of Christian courtesy and fellowship between congregations. At its best, it took the issue of accountability as well as Christian commendation seriously, and I can still recall the sense of welcome and affection which such an introduction generated.

Paul's mockery, however, is targeted at something quite different. The testimonials to which he refers were carefully crafted by the false teachers – written and signed by themselves. So it was no surprise when in fact they met their own standards! We can sometimes be in danger of falling into the same trap. Churches can compare themselves with others according to certain criteria, or can have within them particular groups which define what is truly spiritual. As James Denney expressed it, 'They constitute a religious coterie, a sort of clique or ring in the church, ignoring all but themselves, making themselves the only standard of what is Christian.' In the UK in the 1990s we used to speak of the seventeen different tribes of evangelicalism, and doubtless the number has increased.

The real test of authenticity in Christian ministry is not what kind of testimonial we can write for ourselves. It is not the kind of website our church puts up, or how impressive the glossy publicity might be. I am afraid it has very little to do with titles and ranks within the ecclesiastical hierarchies of Christendom, which are frequently (and mistakenly) employed to commend a leader. Rather, the test will be the abiding fruit of our work demonstrated by lives changed, churches established and Christians making headway in the faith.

So Paul argues the case by explaining the foundation for his 'boasting'. It helps us to understand what true ambition in Christian service should look like.

The foundation for the Lord's commendation

Here Paul demonstrates once again that he is a man of integrity: he will not boast of work which he did not achieve. Rather, the evidence of his apostleship is seen in the 'field' of operations God gave him (10:13). The word for 'field' can also be translated 'measure', so could mean a 'measured area'. So Paul is possibly describing the territory which was his special responsibility. This was the result of the division of labour which is referred to in Galatians 2, and for Paul it included Corinth. It is the field that 'God has assigned to us' (10:13). This was why he poured his energies into his apostolic labours, why he invested so much in seeking to establish the church in Corinth, and why he now felt so distraught at the thought of the church rejecting not only its apostle but potentially the gospel itself.

He might also mean that, if you are boasting about something, it is important that you have a proper 'measure' by which to assess it. So Paul could be saying that he truly does measure up as far as his claims to apostleship are concerned.[5] The evidence of his apostleship was the fact that he had brought the gospel to them. If he had not arrived at Corinth, then of course there would be no foundation for his boasting. 'We are not going too far in our boasting, as would be the case if we had not come to you, for we did get as far as you with the gospel of Christ' (10:14). The believers in Corinth knew how he had laboured amongst them; their very existence as a church was due to his efforts.

There is no need to steal the praise that belongs to others. It is always ugly, of course, and never achieves what we hope for. Instead, we simply need to be true to our God-given calling. In Paul's case, the Christians in Corinth were sufficient evidence of God's grace at work. They were his testimonial, as he said earlier in the letter (3:2).

Again, it is sobering to read these verses, since it is all too easy to take credit for the work of others. This is another aspect of integrity to which we need to keep alert. I recently asked a friend how things were in a city where I used to live, and was told that more and more churches were being established in a small city that does not need them. Often such new churches are made up of the disaffected from elsewhere, built on what we sometimes call 'transfer' growth. It seems very close to taking credit for the hard work of others. Or perhaps a leader is praised for a piece of work when in fact the effort mostly came from a hard-working team, whether colleagues, an assistant, or even his or her family members. It is easy to keep quiet, taking the adulation and credit which more properly belongs to others.

The antidote is to be true to what God has called us to do. If we are faithful in that task, we will not feel the need to be looking over our shoulder at what others are doing, or be anxiously seeking the plaudits of others. Rather, 'we make it our goal to please him' (2 Cor. 5:9).

Our true ambition

The focus of Paul's ministry in the closing verses of 2 Corinthians 10 demonstrates his missionary priorities. His hope was that his ministry could continue in Corinth, and he refers to two significant potential developments: consolidation and mission. Having begun the work, it was vital that it continued. He wanted to see their faith continue to grow (10:15).

This was central to Paul's missionary strategy, as he explains to other churches. He was concerned with depth as well as breadth, with consolidation as well as extension. He wanted to see mature congregations made up of godly disciples, not just statistics of the number of converts in each city. This remains part of the integrity of Christian mission today, and is an essential element of our work. Evangelism, church-planting and the nurturing of congregations to maturity is an organic whole, and Paul's mission included the entire spectrum from initial proclamation to mature Christian discipleship.

However, in contrast to the self-centred claims of Paul's critics in Corinth, with their inflated egos, neatly typed testimonials and persistent self-commendation, Paul quotes from Jeremiah to press home his point. If you are going to boast about anything, do not focus on your own achievements. Do not glory in your work for the Lord, but glory in the Lord of the work. 'Let him who boasts boast in the Lord' (10:17). What really matters in Christian service is the Lord's approval: 'For it is not the one who commends himself who is approved, but the one whom the Lord commends' (10:18).

This is the reward that really matters, the ambition of godly leaders: not the rewards of human status and success, but the Lord's commendation. Some of us might be tempted to be proud of our achievements as Christians, or to see our gifts or status within the Christian community as providing important personal fulfilment and evidence of our commendation as valued church members. Some of our churches or organizations might be tempted to publish success stories of great achievements, glad to be known as centres of Christian excellence and secretly proud of our effective ministry. For all of us tempted to think in this way, Paul reminds us that 'it is not the one who commends himself who is approved'. There are many churches which do not make the Christian newspapers, which have no glossy image, but which are consistently faithful in working for the Lord in a tough environment with little obvious reward.

Writing on the subject of success, Jim Packer suggests:

> Orienting all Christian action to visible success as its goal, a move which to many moderns seems supremely sensible and businesslike, is thus more a weakness in the church than it is a strength; it is a seedbed both for unspiritual vainglory for the self-rated succeeders and of unspiritual despair for the self-rated failures, and a source of shallowness and superficiality all round . . . In the final analysis we do not and cannot know the measure of success as God sees it. Wisdom says: leave success ratings to God, and live your Christianity as a religion of faithfulness rather than an idolatry of achievement.[6]

In all churches there are Christians who are quietly serving Christ, often working very sacrificially and usually without recognition, acknowledgment or thanks. Is it really worthwhile? To such Christians, Paul's words should be a deep encouragement: the real reward is the Lord's commendation. They may not talk about themselves, but they will receive what really matters.

A friend of ours has just died and, after a lifetime of Christian service, the email news came to us with the words of Paul, written as he too came to the end of his life. 'I have fought the good fight, I have finished the race, I have kept the faith. Now there is in store for me the crown of righteousness, which the Lord, the righteous Judge, will award to me on that day – and not only to me, but also to all who have longed for his appearing' (2 Tim. 4:7–8).

The ultimate reward – and therefore the true ambition – for all involved in Christian service is to hear the Lord say, 'Well done, good and faithful servant!' (Matt. 25:21).

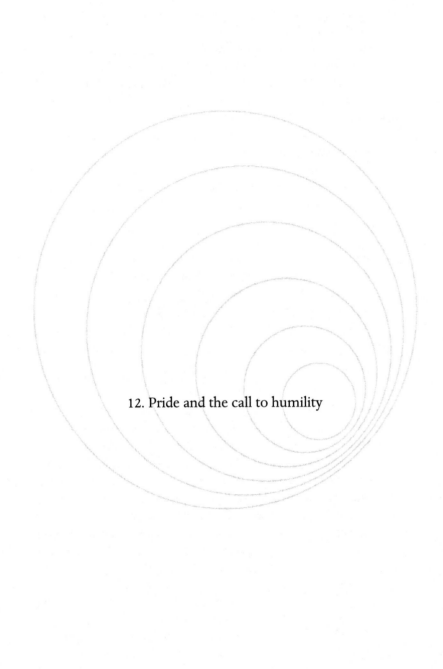

12. Pride and the call to humility

Many years ago, David Christie suggested that Christian ministers face three temptations: 'to recline, to shine and to whine'. They are certainly thought-provoking! But there is one severe temptation in all Christian service, particularly if God grants us a measure of success, and that is to become self-seeking. Our motives become distorted and our ministry loses integrity. We constantly face the insidious enemy of Christian service – the sin of pride.

Eugene Peterson made an astute observation in an article on the subject of 'vocational holiness'.

> Any Christian is at risk in any of the temptations. But those of us who do work explicitly defined as Christian – pastors, teachers, missionaries, chaplains – live in an especially hazardous environment, for the very nature of the work is a constant temptation to sin. The sin is, to put an old word on it, pride. But it is often nearly impossible to identify pride, especially in its early stages. It looks and feels like energetic commitment, sacrificial zeal, selfless devotion. We become Christians because we are convinced that we need a Saviour. But the minute we enter into a life of ministry we set about acting on behalf of the Saviour.[1]

Boasting is a repeated theme in Paul's writing, and in 2 Corinthians 11 we encounter the legitimate focus of Christian boasting. 'If I must boast, I will boast of the things that show my weakness' (11:30). As we have seen, Paul faced opponents who doubted his claims to apostleship and who boasted of their own superior qualifications and spiritual experiences. These so-called super-apostles were capturing the minds and hearts of the Corinthian believers, and Paul was concerned that the church should not be led astray. The serious side to the issue was not so much the distasteful nature of boasting, ugly though that was. It was the assumptions that lay beneath the surface. The false teachers saw their pedigree and spiritual experience as the foundation for their life and potential influence. Far from trusting Christ and his gospel, they boasted about their ancestry or their spiritual lives or their human skills. Their boasting therefore represented a betrayal of all that Paul had taught the Corinthians about the gospel.

In describing the main features of his ministry he was particularly anxious to help the Corinthians see the foundations of that calling.

What qualified him to serve them? In an extraordinary list of 'achievements', Paul provides a CV in chapter 11 which demonstrates that weakness was the main characteristic of his apostleship. It is the absolute opposite of what his opponents might expect. Yet it was deliberate, for boasting about weakness inevitably pointed away from himself to other priorities – the priorities of Christ. There was no room for pride for the person who knew he had been saved by grace.

Instead of recording his great victories, it is a catalogue of his sufferings. Instead of proclaiming his great strengths, it exposes his weaknesses. Reading it through as it stands has its own impact, bowling us over as we see the range and intensity of the suffering he endured as an apostle. The importance of this section of 2 Corinthians for Christian integrity should not be underestimated. How will God help us to overcome our human pride? How will he bring us to our senses and call us to humility? It will nearly always be through crisis, through failure, or through the experience of weakness. These are often the things which God uses to restore our perspective and produce a Christ-like humility.

A big let-down

First, in chapter 11 he lists the multiple occasions when he encountered opposition as he preached the gospel, from imprisonment to flogging. Frequently these experiences brought him close to death. Then he records the various physical dangers which accompanied his many miles of travelling, and lists within that the dangers from bandits and from false brothers. Alongside these perils he suffered the physical and emotional drain of constant hard work, sleep deprivation and the ill-effects of hunger and cold.

In what appears as a short and insignificant postscript, he adds, 'Besides everything else, I face daily the pressure of my concern for all the churches' (11:28). We know a little of that pressure from the Corinthian correspondence. But multiply this several times over, as befits an apostle who founded so many congregations and whose pastoral heart was so large, and we have a further glimpse of the weight of responsibility and sense of pressure which Paul constantly endured.

It is a very compact list, but it does not take too much imagination to reconstruct the sort of lifestyle which this man faced. Unlike the great spiritual leaders of the day, held in such esteem by the Corinthian super-apostles, Paul recounts no stories of his victories, tells no stories of admiring crowds, lists no prestigious lectureships. He deliberately chooses to major on his weaknesses. He is no bionic superman, no spiritual guru, no hero in the classic traditions of the day. He is tired and bruised, an itinerant preacher of a foolish message. He presses home the point in verse 30. If he is forced to boast of his achievements and sing his praises in the manner of the false teachers, then he will sing from a very different songsheet: 'I will boast of the things that show my weakness.'

His final illustration in chapter 11 adds a further touch of irony. In his list of 'achievements' he adds the example of his hurried and ignominious departure from Damascus. The city was being guarded in the hope of capturing Paul, but he was dropped over the wall in a basket and once he hit the ground he legged it away from Damascus as fast as he could. The great hero Paul! Would you have boasted about that kind of humiliating exit? It certainly did not match the Corinthians' expectations of the leaders of the day. But Paul must have had a twinkle in his eye as he told the story and rounded off his autobiography. How about that one for an example on his CV! But it was an illustration of the key to his life: God's power being demonstrated in Paul's weakness.

We can learn from this in our own culture, which, like first-century Greek culture, mocks the fool and despises the weak. We must learn to gain the perspective of this letter. We might be tempted to think that God can only use the big programmes or the successful churches or the articulate preachers. Or we might feel that our work is weak and insignificant, so God cannot possibly use us as much as he uses others. But the paradox of Christian experience tells us something different: God was at work in the apparent weakness of Jesus on the cross, and in the apparent foolishness of Paul's experience. So he continues, 'I must go on boasting' (12:1).

Up and away
A further element in the Corinthians' expectation of what constitutes a truly spiritual leader related to profound, mystical, otherworldly experiences. The false teachers fostered the delusion that, in line with the culture of the day, the leaders worthy of respect were those

who seemed to walk several feet above the ground – people whose spiritual life was mysterious and heavenly, full of visions and ecstatic revelations.

Paul felt that there was 'nothing to be gained' by boasting of such experiences (12:1), and for him to join in such boasting truly was foolish. But he wanted to demonstrate some important principles for the Corinthians, who were in danger of being captivated by the dramatic stories of spiritual exaltation, as if these constituted the essential elements of Christian life and leadership. Indeed, Paul's reluctance to tell his own story is further underlined by his writing style. 'I know a man,' he says (12:2), not wishing to be too up-front about it. Such modesty is important for us to note in our world too, which shares with first-century Greek culture a sense of awe – even gullible superstition – when it comes to stories of remarkable visions.

First, Paul's experience was so overwhelming that he was unable to describe it accurately. He was at a loss to find adequate vocabulary and he could not easily fit the experience within his usual theological grid. Where did it take place? He was not sure (12:2–4). Was it in the body or out of the body? He did not know (12:2–3). What spiritual messages did he receive? He could not say (12:4). Despite all the uncertainties and qualifications, we can be sure that this was a profound moment, etched deeply on his memory. He was 'caught up' into paradise. We should never be cynical about the possibility of such an experience, for God has his purposes in the lives of those called to unique areas of ministry. While we are not told why Paul had such an experience, it was real enough – 'God knows,' Paul repeats (12:2, 3).

Nevertheless, we should notice a second feature of the experience: it was highly unusual. Paul did not expect such experiences to be part of the normal Christian life. It had occurred fourteen years ago (12:2), and presumably Paul had no more recent examples to call on. So while we should not be dismissive of such an experience, neither should we use this passage to argue that it should be a regular occurrence, nor even expected for any other Christian.

Third, he underlines once again his reluctance to speak about the experience (12:5). I am not sure we would have been so reticent. These days we might have been tempted to secure a publisher, or be profiled in Christian magazines, or make a DVD, or go on tour. But Paul is reluctant: 'I will boast about a man like that, but I will not boast about myself, except about my weaknesses' (12:5). In his book, boasting about extraordinary spiritual visions as a basis for his calling was utterly foolish. His concern was that he should be judged not on the basis of ecstatic experiences, but on the basis of his words and actions. Here again is an example of Paul's fundamental integrity. 'I refrain [from boasting], so no one will think more of me than is warranted by what I do or say' (12:6).

Paul saw one great danger with such a spiritual experience, and that was the danger of the sin of pride entering his life because of the 'surpassingly great revelations'. He is careful to point out that, 'To keep me from becoming conceited because of these surpassingly great revelations, there was given me a thorn in my flesh, a messenger of Satan, to torment me' (12:7).

A big pain

There has been a great deal of speculation about what this thorn might have been. Literally the word means a 'splinter' or a 'stake'. It is intended to convey the idea of excruciating pain (such as being impaled on a stake). It is not simply a nagging irritation. Some writers suggest it was a physical weakness of some sort, perhaps malaria, epilepsy, migraine, a speech impediment, or an unimpressive bodily presence. Others suggest it was opposition, or spiritual temptation, or the shame of persecution by the Jews. Perhaps the strongest case can be made for a form of eye trouble, with various clues given us from the letter to the Galatians.[2] But we cannot come to a conclusion, and it is a good thing that we cannot. If he had spelt it out, those of us without that particular weakness might have missed the force of his teaching. It might be a job that God has given us to do which feels deeply uncomfortable, even painful; it might be a relationship we have to face, or physical or mental pressure in our Christian service, or a weakness we see within ourselves which the devil exploits.

In such circumstances we frequently ask ourselves about the source of the affliction. Is it chance, or fate? Is it Satanic, or is it entirely neutral, part of what it means to be human? Paul writes, 'There was given me a thorn in my flesh, a messenger of Satan, to torment me' (12:7). It is clear from the New Testament that Paul experienced Satanic resistance in his ministry. We have seen in 2 Corinthians 4 that the god of this world is actively at work, blinding the minds of unbelievers. Now Paul states here that the thorn in his flesh was part of Satan's harassment, or buffeting. But the context also shows us that this was not out of control. Like Job, this situation was still under the Lord's oversight and care.

It is important we affirm that nothing lies outside the scope of God's sovereignty and control, not even Satan. It is clear that Satan is limited in his power. He can only act within the parameters which God has set. Even the worst of Satan's activities may be redeemed by God to fulfil his own purposes. Significantly, in Job's story the Lord draws the lines. 'The LORD said to Satan, "Very well, then, he is in your hands; but you must spare his life." So Satan went out from the presence of the LORD and afflicted Job with painful sores from the soles of his feet to the top of his head' (Job 2:6).

Even the work of Satan, Paul testifies, is overruled so that it assists in bringing about God's good purposes. I found a very helpful illustration in the writing of a German pastor and theologian, Helmut Thielicke, who preached on the Lord's Prayer in Germany during World War II, as bombs were falling on his city.

> Everything God permits the dark powers to do must first pass in review before him. It is as if God intercepts these originally evil and disastrous missiles of fate, catches them in his fatherly arms, and sends them in the direction he wants them to go for the benefit of his children. We can confidently accept even the hardest blows when we know that his good hand is at work in our lives.[3]

We are to live as faithful children of the Father, who is the Sovereign Lord. God's purpose is not to bypass difficulties, but to transform them. In Paul's case there is no doubt why the messenger of Satan was allowed: 'In order to prevent me becoming absurdly conceited,' as J. B. Phillips expresses it. Perhaps it is the major hindrance in our Christian service. Pride seeks to take the glory which properly belongs to God. Personal ambition, the love of prestige and popularity – it is no wonder that God also allows us a thorn, to keep us humble and to keep us fruitful in his service.

When I was five years old I contracted polio, leaving me mildly disabled. It is a very small affliction, one that these days I hardly notice. But I realize how important this has been in pushing me to depend on

God and also to depend on others. There are things we shall learn about ourselves and about the Lord which we would never otherwise learn. It builds spiritual muscle and inserts vertebrae in our spines. And as Paul states in 2 Corinthians 1, it also equips us to support others who are under pressure in the Christian family. So we should not miss the opportunity. The purpose of these challenges is that we learn the lesson of Paul's theme text, 'power is made perfect in weakness'.

'Three times I pleaded with the Lord to take it away from me' (12:8). If weakness has no other purpose than to turn us to God in prayer, it has performed a valuable function. It may not be fashionable to admit it in our culture, and it probably was not appreciated by the super-apostles in Corinth either. We are meant to be self-assured, self-confident, independent. Many of us identify with Paul's situation. Something is embedded in our lives which means 'our stride becomes a limp'. Even in the midst of our genuine attempts to serve God, we wince with the pain. It is then that we appeal to God to help us. Paul did not succumb to passive resignation. He did not throw in the towel. Instead, he says in verse 8, 'Three times I pleaded with the Lord to take it away from me.' What answer did he receive? 'But he said to me, "My grace is sufficient for you, for my power is made perfect in weakness"' (12:9).

In such circumstances we repeatedly turn to God, because God is the only one who can help. We realize that weakness is the place where we cease to be self-reliant, and turn instead to the God of the resurrection – and we come to see the bigger picture, the purpose behind the pain. 'This happened that we might not rely on ourselves but on God, who raises the dead' (1:9). This is often how the Lord graciously helps us with the temptation to pride. Whatever our circumstances, pride is never far away. Writing about pastoral ministry in the church, Michael Ramsay said, 'If you do well, you can be pleased with yourself, and humility is in peril. If you do badly, you may worry about yourself, and humility is in peril. If people are nice to you and tell you what a good clergyman you are, humility is in peril. If people are nasty to you, you have a grievance and humility is in peril.'[4]

All of us face the temptation to pride; none of us should be surprised by God's solution.

Down is up

Paul's personal story indicates that, by God's grace, evil never has the final word. His affliction confronted his pride and pushed him to humble dependence. 'He said to me, "My grace is sufficient for you, for my power is made perfect in weakness"' (12:9). It was an unexpected answer to his prayer which became the inspiration of his life. Now God's all-sufficient grace was poured into his life, not in spite of the thorn, but because of that very weakness. Now he experienced Christ's power in a way he never would have done without walking this pathway. Now he could say to the Corinthians that the foundation for his apostleship was not the proud boasting of Jewish heritage or ecstatic spiritual experience, but the heart of the gospel itself.

In all Christian service the example of Jesus stands before us. He laid aside his rights and privileges. He took a bowl to wash the feet of his followers. He submitted to the mockery and cruelty of petty officials. He felt the pain of Roman nails. We can search the Gospel records and we will not find a hint of pride. He served his Father with obedience and his disciples with humility. As those who seek to follow the Master, pride will have no place. We know we are dependent entirely on the grace of God and the power of Christ. Paul's thorn is a reminder that Christian leadership is a call to humility, and that the Lord will find his gracious way of keeping that uppermost in our minds as we serve him.

Section D – Over to you ...

- What aspects of a leader's power might go to your head, and how can you handle these with integrity?
- In what ways are Christian leaders tempted to boost their ego, build their reputation or climb the ladder? How can you respond to these temptations with a greater ruthlessness?
- What are the positive aspects of ambition which need to be nurtured in Christian service?
- You might not be blatant in your boasting, but what are the subtle ways in which you parade your gifts, experience or knowledge?

- Accepting a thorn in the flesh could lead to passivity or even paralysis. How does Paul's testimony encourage you to keep stretching hard in your Christian service, in the midst of weakness?

E. Integrity as a way of life

13. Living contentedly

It is estimated by the European Union that anxiety is responsible for the loss of more man hours at work than all the infectious diseases put together. It is the result of many factors: it might be 'modernity stress', arising from our sense of obligation to squeeze more and more into less time; or the incessant drive towards materialism, with our consumer appetite longing to possess more, enjoy more and relax more; or it might be the inevitable impact of relational breakdown, the fracture of marriages and communities across the continent, from which few of us are immune. Living a life of settled contentment, whatever our circumstances, is rarely achieved.

The situation is not always much better in our Christian service. While we might hope to distance ourselves from the distracted restlessness of our culture, a balanced contentment, a quiet spirit and a calm strength frequently seem elusive. We are worried about managing our 'time budget', or making up for 'lost time'; we live under the stressful pressure of the immediate. We are aware that in Christian ministry we live with the pressure of constant opportunity, with far more to do than we can manage. We often carry our work with us, and we now live in an age of what a Microsoft researcher called 'continuous partial attention'. It means that while you are answering your email and talking to your child, your mobile rings and you have another conversation. You are now involved in a continuous flow of interactions in which you can only partially concentrate on each. The bad news is that you are never 'out' any more. The assumption is that you are always in, always accessible.

In Christian service we also feel we are coping with the constant expenditure of time and emotion, and the challenge of multiple jobs in our work, our church and our family. There are many times when our patience is stretched to the limit and our personal resources seem completely inadequate. The expectations or demands of other people impact our motives. Both applause and criticism can knock us off course, and the pressures of our work push us to less than godly behaviour. Paul's catalogues of suffering put our own into perspective, for few of us confront the range and intensity of difficulty which he encountered. Nonetheless, we know how our circumstances and emotional responses can impact not only our own sense of well-being, but the way in which we carry out our Christian service.

Although we may not always realize it, the way in which we

respond to pressures also has its impact on others. In 2 Corinthians 6 Paul demonstrates how he responded in a range of demanding settings, but first he alerts us to the potential impact of our attitudes and behaviour on those around us.

Road blocks or bridges?

In verses 3 and 4 he highlights two opposites: 'We put no stumbling-block in anyone's path, so that our ministry will not be discredited. Rather, as servants of God we commend ourselves in every way' (6:3).

He is describing two possibilities. Either we are laying road blocks, by which the gospel is discredited, or we are building bridges, by which the gospel is commended. He explains how, in a wide variety of circumstances, he has sought to carry out his apostolic ministry. He is deeply concerned that his ministry should not be 'discredited' (6:3), a word which conveys the idea of mocking and ridicule. As we have seen throughout 2 Corinthians, Paul was defending his ministry as he faced a range of criticisms – that he was not at all impressive as an apostle, that he was too plain and straightforward as a preacher. He has responded by declaring that he is not a salesman, a pedlar of God's Word; he is not interested in image, or performance. Instead, 'by setting forth the truth plainly we commend ourselves to every man's conscience in the sight of God' (4:2).

So he is determined to put no obstacle in anyone's path. There should be nothing in his life or ours which would be a 'stumbling-block' to others, holding them back from faith in the gospel or from progress in their discipleship. It would be deeply disturbing if someone failed to become a Christian not because of the offence of the cross, but because of our inconsistent behaviour.

When I was ten, I was involved in a small north London church. One day I experienced the shock of discovering failure in the Christian community. The treasurer had embezzled funds for several years. In a small church the impact was considerable, especially on young Christians like myself. A prominent Christian leader had deceived people; someone we had seen as beyond failure had acted inconsistently. In many churches such failure can paralyze the Christian community and can inhibit growth. In fact, by God's grace, failure in our church was handled in a gracious and firm manner. The brother was eventually restored, and with great humility served in the church in mundane tasks for many years. I came to respect him enormously. But I learned some important lessons as a young believer: that we must pray for leaders, all of whom are vulnerable; that those who claim to follow Christ must live his life; and that God can redeem failure.

Paul is reinforcing the fact that his message and his ministry were wedded to a godly life that made the gospel credible and believable. So now Paul refers not to discrediting the gospel, but to 'commending' his ministry (6:4). He demonstrates how his life matched his profession in a range of tough situations, which he now lists in one of several catalogues that appear in his letter. If his critics want to know what really commends an apostle, or any servant of Christ, he now tells them. He would not get many nods of approval from the super-apostles in Corinth for this particular list, but he wanted to underline that this is what it means to follow the Servant King, the crucified Messiah. And it introduces us to the importance of living contentedly.

It is beautifully expressed, almost hymn-like in its quality. But it is a list full of paradox, like clashing musical notes that cry out for resolution, as Tom Wright expresses it. In that sense it is similar to Paul's writing in 2 Corinthians 4, where weakness and power, life and death, are juxtaposed. There are at least three qualities to notice.

Patient endurance
He begins with what one early writer called a 'blizzard of troubles'. He lists three groups of three trials which he faced, each 'in great endurance' (6:4), and his purpose is to demonstrate the genuine integrity of his ministry. The first three pressures are described in general terms: 'troubles, hardships and distresses' (6:4). Then he describes three specific pressures inflicted by others: 'beatings, imprisonments and riots' (6:5). Finally, he lists three which were self-imposed: 'hard work, sleepless nights and hunger' (6:5). In these ways, remarkably, he 'commends' his ministry (6:4). He deliberately includes the words 'in every way' – there is no exception. Everything about his life and ministry is characterized by integrity.

In chapter 12 we saw that Paul did not want to be guilty of the boasting which characterized his opponents in Corinth, with their pride in physical appearance and in heroic achievements. As far as Paul was concerned, if he had to boast he would boast about his weaknesses (11:30). Here he indicates that the best way of judging the consistency of his ministry was to watch how he responded to pressures of every kind. Whatever the circumstances, and however extreme the pressure, he sought to remain steady in his patient endurance. This was the way to commend true Christian ministry. We should often pray for the gift of perseverance, for we encounter times when we wish to throw in the towel, when it seems best to move to another church, to change jobs, or to abandon the project. An important element of living with contentment is the capacity to understand God's call and then to endure patiently.

Complete consistency
The next set of expressions (6:6–7) describe the qualities with which he sought to carry out his work. They are each the result of the Holy Spirit's ministry, for he is the one who produces the harvest of qualities which Paul lists. Again they underline that here is a man whose ministry was consistent. There is no sales talk, no propaganda, no manipulation, but a consistent life and a clear message, 'in truthful speech and in the power of God' (6:7). Notice the emphasis on moral blamelessness, on right relationships – 'purity, understanding, patience and kindness' (6:6).

These are the things which authenticate our ministry. However eloquent my preaching, however impressive my commanding presence as a leader, without these qualities I am not an authentic servant of the gospel. As J. B. Phillips paraphrases verse 7, 'Our sole defence is a life of integrity.'

This kind of modelling is important whatever work God calls you to. One of my relatives once worked at a theological college, serving on the kitchen staff every Saturday to earn some pocket money. Quite often she had a story to tell of how rude or discourteous one or other of the students had been to her and to the girls who served the food or cleaned the tables. She even threatened to email the churches where the ordinands hoped to serve, giving them an unsolicited reference concerning their behaviour! Well, on the one hand, it was not too significant; we can all be grumpy at breakfast, after all. On the other, I found myself helping a younger Christian to make sense of the less than godly behaviour of people who are preparing to serve the church.

I choose this example deliberately. It is often in these ordinary situations that the quality and integrity of our lives is most evident.

Most of us will not face the range of pressures which Paul lists in his catalogue here in 2 Corinthians 6, but we will all know the trigger points in our lives which make it hard to live as the gospel demands. Most of us need to keep alert to the dangers of inconsistent responses when we are particularly tired. Some of us find criticism extremely difficult to handle, and are sharp in our defensive reactions. Some of us need words of approval to remain energized, and find it hard to stay on course when there is no feedback or support. Others struggle to be patient when we have perfectionist tendencies, and colleagues fail to deliver to the standard we expect.

We will look more fully at the theme of consistency in the next chapter, but we should note that, given the context of Paul's writing here is one of extreme pressure, it is all the more remarkable that he 'commends' his ministry – and therefore the gospel itself – in these ways. Each quality that Paul lists is worthy of prayerful reflection. How do we express *purity* – in relationships with others, in sexual thought and behaviour, in the handling of money? Are we known both for our *patience* and our *kindness*? And is our love *sincere* and unhypocritical (6:6)? Do we sustain our commitment, in whatever situation, to speak *the word of truth*? That is, are our lives and ministries shaped by gospel priorities?

In case we should feel crushed by such a standard, we need to notice again that the list includes *the Holy Spirit* and *the power of God*. All the qualities listed here are God-given. This is significant in relation to the issue of suffering, as we saw from Paul's testimony in 2 Corinthians 12. That is, suffering itself is of no merit. We do not rejoice in sufferings for their own sake, but because pressures (such as Paul has listed here in chapter 6) are the occasion for the experience of God's power. In that sense it is no surprise that Paul can record these qualities as characteristic of his ministry in the midst of all his troubles. They are the result of the Holy Spirit's empowering presence.

We should not miss this, for two reasons. First, it helps us to see that we are not engaged in self-commendation. We know what Paul thinks about that from his comments in 2 Corinthians 10, which we looked at earlier. He refuses to engage in self-commendation, and objects to such behaviour on the part of the pseudo-apostles. Rather, as we live in this way, empowered by the Spirit, we are commending the gospel itself. We are reflecting the dying and rising life of Jesus.

Second, we could easily buckle in our work if we concluded that such qualities – purity, patience, kindness, genuine love – were simply down to our self-discipline. For sure, determined resolution is needed. In Galatians 5 Paul is clear enough: we adopt a ruthless attitude and we must 'crucify the flesh with its passions and desires'. But this is complemented by the call to 'live by the Spirit' and to 'keep in step with the Spirit' (Gal. 5:16–26). As we live in conscious awareness of the Spirit's presence and work in our lives, so the harvest of qualities – the fruit of the Spirit – will increasingly characterize our daily lives.

Settled contentment

I recently attended a conference for pastors and lay preachers where we studied the theme of Christian ministry together. There I met a group of men who proposed the idea that, for a Christian leader to have any credibility, a degree of outward success was necessary. They were not buying into everything which so-called prosperity theology proclaims, but they did suggest that dressing well and having a reasonable car and an appropriate title were all necessary elements of a leadership style which won an audience. For sure, I would not want to speak against appropriate social behaviour, and there is no point in creating unnecessary offence. But what are we to make of their suggestion?

Paul's final cluster of qualities gives us some significant pointers. Again they illustrate the stresses and strains which characterized his ministry.

> . . . through glory and dishonour, bad report and good report; genuine, yet regarded as impostors; known, yet regarded as unknown; dying, and yet we live on; beaten, and yet not killed; sorrowful, yet always rejoicing; poor, yet making many rich; having nothing, and yet possessing everything. (6:8–10)

Whether people praised him or mocked him, whether they welcomed him or rejected him, whatever the circumstances of his life, Paul had gained God's perspective. His value system was shaped by the values of God's kingdom, not the values of this world. It was all to do with perspective.

It is very easy for our circumstances or for the expectations of others around us to control our lives. If we are honest, we will admit that our self-esteem is often bound up with our popularity ratings, or our status, or our income. However self-assured we might be, when some of these things are stripped away from our lives we can see how much of our identity as individuals is bound up with them. That is why, for many people of our generation, the loss of jobs or position can be so devastating. I read recently of one despairing businessman who said, 'For thirty years I've been climbing a ladder, only to discover that it's propped against the wrong wall.' But Paul asserts in verses 8 and 9 that, even when he is dishonoured, or when he is the target of a smear campaign, or ignored as an unknown, or regarded as an impostor, or living with nothing to his name, he seeks to live with humble contentment.

In a world which thinks very differently, we can easily be tempted to compromise our faith or dilute our Christian witness. Christian leaders can easily succumb to the world's pressures. We need to hold the things of this world lightly, for if we are concerned with our own reputation or honour, with material comfort and security, then it is unlikely that we will live a life worthy of the gospel. Our ministry will be 'discredited' and, instead of encouraging others forward, we will be placing a road block across their path. But true servants of God, filled with his Spirit, will seek to live lives which are consistent with the gospel they proclaim. It was a radical statement in the Greek world of Paul's day, and it will be just as radical today. If we judge Christians by the superficial criteria of our world – titles, clothes, bank balance – we have missed what really matters. Our calling to serve Christ is likely to be very different. It might cost us our comfort, our security, or our health, and maybe even our family or life itself. We do not measure the effectiveness of leaders by the indices of worldly success, but by their conformity to the way of the cross.

Do you recall Paul's testimony in Philippians 4:11–13? He expresses the same sense of balanced contentment, whether in need or in plenty. He had 'learned to be content', and that was because he had discovered God's resources. 'I can do everything through him who gives me strength.' Christian contentment is not dependent on outward circumstances, not even on a successful Christian ministry. It arises from our fellowship with Christ. Then I can meet all circumstances with contentment, Paul says.

One simple image from the Wisdom literature reinforces the point. The Teacher in Ecclesiastes describes, first, the bondage of non-stop competition: 'I saw that all labour and all achievement spring from man's envy of his neighbour. This too is meaningless, a chasing after the wind' (Eccl. 4:4). In the next verse he describes the opposite: self-destructive idleness. 'The fool folds his hands and ruins himself' (4:5). But there follows a beautiful expression that sums up true wisdom in life: 'Better one handful with tranquillity than two handfuls with toil and chasing after the wind' (4:6). 'A handful of quietness', 'one handful with tranquillity'. We are content with what we have and are not grasping for more. We are not tempted to define our identity by what we do, or what we have, or what we achieve. The heart of the matter is bowing to the will of God, trusting him more fully and acknowledging his good purposes for our lives.

The verses we have looked at in 2 Corinthians 6 have been called Paul's apostolic ID card. We commend our ministry, we honour Christ, when we seek to live like this too. Integrity as a way of life means living contentedly whatever our circumstances. It means that we rely on God's resources, live under his watchful eye and enjoy his fatherly care.

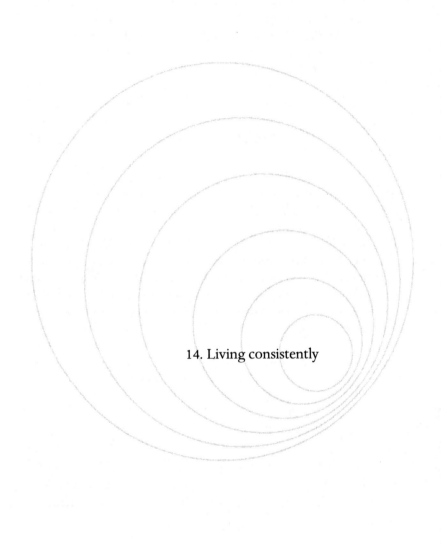

14. Living consistently

The writer Dallas Willard tells the story of an American pastor who became very angry at something that was done during a Sunday morning church service. Immediately after the service he found the person responsible and gave him a merciless rebuke. Unfortunately he was still wearing his radio microphone. His angry exchange was broadcast over the entire church building – apparently even in the Sunday school rooms and the car park. 'Soon afterwards he moved to another church,' Willard comments dryly.[1]

It would be humorous were it not for the fact that we know many of us in Christian ministry live by double standards. British newspapers recently carried articles and letters about the moral qualifications for bishops and leaders in the Church of England. One letter from a senior leader in the church said this: 'If all present bishops and priests who have at some time in the past had a sexual relationship with someone – male or female – to whom they were not married, were rejected [from ministry in the church], not more than 2 in 10 would survive.' So he suggests that 80% of leaders in the church are hiding guilty secrets of past inconsistency and moral failure. I am not sure how he carried out his research. But we know that failure to live lives of integrity not only results in a lack of leadership credibility but, more seriously, dishonours the cause of the gospel and the God who calls us into his service.

I like the variation to the well-known phrase – 'we should preach what we practise'. I realize it will drastically reduce the length and variety of my sermons, but it is at the heart of integrity.

The call to a holy life

Let us suppose that you are playing a game of word association. You are given a postcard on which you are invited to write down words that surface in your mind when you hear the word 'holiness'. What would you write down? Here is a list provided by John White some years ago, and maybe you can identify with some of the associations he makes.

Thinness; hollow-eyed gauntness; beards; sandals; long robes; stone cells; no sex; no jokes; hair shirts; frequent cold baths; fasting; hours of prayer; wild rocky deserts; getting up at 4.00 a.m.; clean fingernails; stained glass; self-humiliation.[2]

What do you think? It's strangely religious, isn't it? And sadly that is what the word has come to mean. It is associated with painful and rigorous effort, with withdrawal from normal life, with the world of the weird and wacky religious fanatic. This is one reason why we discuss the subject less and less. It is not on our agenda these days. David Wilkinson, scientist and Christian apologist, points out that if you advertise a talk on 'The Christian view of sex' or 'Healing in the power of the Spirit' you can guarantee an excited, packed congregation. A talk on holiness may receive the same enthusiasm as 'Advanced tax returns – for very sad people'. Holiness gets a bad press. When a British publisher brought out a new edition of the Bible they simply called it 'The Bible', and a spokesman said, 'We dropped the word "holy" to give it a more mass market appeal.'

The truth of the matter is that holiness is not to be locked away as a religious word of limited relevance to our lives. Holiness is to shape who we are. It should describe everything about us – our identity, our attitude, our behaviour, our corporate life as God's distinct people. It has to do with the everyday, with the mundane of our daily lives, so that it removes any distinction between the so-called sacred and the secular. It describes who we are and what we are to become.

The call to live consistently
In 2 Corinthians 6, Paul continues the theme of integrity as a way of life which we looked at in the last chapter. Here he approaches it from a variety of directions. In the section beginning at verse 14 he addresses the theme negatively: 'Do not be yoked together with unbelievers.' This is a picture borrowed from the book of Deuteronomy. Here the law forbids ploughing a field using two different animals working together. An ox and a donkey would obviously pull at different speeds and so there is no point in harnessing them together. This was one example of several instances in Old Testament law where God's people were required to act consistently. There should be no mixing of crops in the field, no mixing of different fibres in their cloth and, for the people themselves, no contamination through inappropriate association with their pagan neighbours. It reflected God's concern that his people should be set apart, living their lives by his standards.

Paul urges the Corinthians to live in this distinct, undivided way, and the command of verse 14 is quite pointed: 'Do not be yoked together with unbelievers.' To press it home he asks a series of five rhetorical questions (6:14–16). Each question demonstrates that trying to combine secular and Christian values is like trying to mix oil and water: they are completely incompatible.

Paul then addresses the subject positively. He again reinforces his case with a well-known Old Testament theme, using a phrase which was common to God's covenant promise: 'For we are the temple of the living God. As God has said, "I will live with them and walk among them, and I will be their God, and they will be my people" ' (6:16). His point is this: how can you belong to God and then at the same time flirt with the world? This is part of Paul's continuing concern that the Corinthians should resist the temptation to adopt the false values of the new teachers in town. Consistent believers would not give house room to 'idols', he implies in verse 16; they would reject any such secular intrusion, because their lives and their Christian community were the home of the living God. We are the temple of God and the family of God. He lives with us and we belong to him.

Paul takes still more ammunition from his Old Testament arsenal with the strong call to holiness from the prophets: 'Come out from them and be separate' (6:17). Since these verses have sometimes been misused, it is important to understand that Paul is not arguing for a withdrawal from the world. He has spoken in chapter 5 of the calling to be ambassadors who are sent into the world. We do not automatically withdraw when we become members of God's family. We are given the responsibility to live distinct Christian lives, proclaiming the gospel of reconciliation in the midst of a fallen world. But, like Jesus, Paul is urging us to keep our 'saltiness', not to take on the values and ambitions of the world. In the context of Corinth it seems he was especially anxious to address the challenge of paganism and idolatry, as his final question implies: 'What agreement is there between the temple of God and idols?' (6:16).

This passage has frequently been used to explain why Christians should avoid inappropriate partnerships – not to be unequally yoked, for example, in marriage or in business. This seems a legitimate application of the principles Paul is seeking to expound. If becoming a Christian means your whole view of life changes – different values, different ambitions, different ethical standards and, most importantly, a different authority in your life – how can you share your life intimately with someone outside God's family? How can you be 'at one'? Or, as Paul expresses it in verse 15, 'What does a believer have in common with an unbeliever?' Painful as it might be initially, Christians are called to avoid any close liaison which will compromise the distinctness of our calling. But we should also underline that this is not a call for the wrong kind of separation. There are many committed Christians who are in a marriage where their spouse is not yet a believer. In these circumstances Paul encourages the Christian to stick with it, as he writes in 1 Corinthians 7. Peter says the same: if you have an unbelieving spouse, the best thing to do is not to withdraw, but to live the life. 'Wives, in the same way be submissive to your husbands so that, if any of them do not believe the word, they may be won over without words by the behaviour of their wives, when they see the purity and reverence of your lives' (1 Pet. 3:1–2).

The call to Christian distinctness

In fact, Paul is simply encouraging Christian saltiness in every area of life. When I was serving amongst university students with IFES (the International Fellowship of Evangelical Students), I heard a story which came from an East Asian graduates conference. One Christian graduate was invited to give his testimony of how he sought to live under Christ's lordship in his business life. He lived in a country where bribery and corruption were endemic. He worked for an electricity supply company and, one day, was approached by two men who offered him money if he would give them a contract. He immediately refused. Some while later they returned, this time threatening violence against him if he refused to award them the contract. Again, he refused. When they visited for the third time, they threatened injury to his wife and children. So he spoke to his family and to the church pastor, and they all agreed that he should stand his ground. When they next came, he said to them, 'I've been saved by the blood of Christ. If you can offer me more than that, I'll take it.' The men were so overwhelmed by that response that they withdrew.

When the graduates at the conference heard this testimony, they stood on their chairs to cheer him. They were so heartened that a Christian was willing to stand up and be counted. They all lived in societies where living consistently can be very costly. And so for us. It might threaten career prospects, or the possibility of marriage, or making the kind of money others make. But if we have experienced God's grace in the gospel, if we belong to him, we will be ready to stand for his cause, ready to display our Christian saltiness. So it is a painful but necessary question. What about our Christian distinctness? We are not simply to endorse secular culture, but to challenge it; we are not just to adopt its values uncritically, but to weigh them up in the light of biblical standards. To what extent is our leadership an echo of the world's aspirations?

The call to commitment

As Paul draws the section to a close, there is a significant word of encouragement. It is a call for radical commitment. 'Since we have these promises, dear friends, let us purify ourselves from everything that contaminates body and spirit, perfecting holiness out of reverence for God' (7:1). What is at stake for the Corinthians, and for all of us who are members of God's family, is not simply the integrity of our witness, but our reverence for God himself. How we behave will reflect on our Father. We are called to purify ourselves 'out of reverence for God'.

In his book *The Trivialization of God*, Donald McCullough writes, 'Reverence and awe have often been replaced by a yawn of familiarity. The consuming fire has been domesticated into a candle flame, adding a bit of religious atmosphere, perhaps, but no heat, no blinding light, no power for purification ... We prefer the illusion of a safer deity, and so we have pared God down to manageable proportions.'[3] Our view of God will determine our manner of life. The teachers of the Old Testament make the point: the *fear of the Lord* is the beginning of wisdom. While we rejoice in the intimacy of a relationship with the God who is our Father, *reverence for God* – an awareness of his utter holiness – might mean that we should at times take a few steps back. Isaiah was overwhelmed as he entered the Lord's temple; Moses was shaken to the core when he met the 'I am'. Perhaps the call to live lives of purity and holiness would take on a new dimension if we knew more of what such godly fear felt like. Such reverence, though, does not make us shrink away. It needs to be seen alongside the wonderful affirmations of God's faithful commitment to us: 'I will live with them and walk among them' (6:16).

There are many things which will drag us away from God's standards, many things which 'contaminate body and spirit' (7:1). So we are encouraged, first, to 'purify ourselves' (7:1). There are some things which need to be pruned away, some elements of our lives that need to be washed clean. This might be facing compromise in a particular relationship; or being at a party which turns in the wrong direction; or when filling out self-assessment tax forms; or in our attitude to someone who has harmed us. It can refer to anything which results in our 'going out of tune' spiritually. Nothing should be allowed to infect our minds, hearts or bodies – it is a position of no compromise, of absolute integrity. The second exhortation is found in the phrase 'perfecting holiness' (7:1). The way Paul constructs his appeal implies that this is our regular, day-by-day responsibility.

In the Old Testament, the way in which the people of God lived their lives was a statement to the neighbouring nations of the kind of God they believed in. Their community life, their economic relationships, their care for the poor, their commitment to worship – the distinctness of their lives was a witness to those around them that they belonged to God. Our task is the same. In our culture most people are weary of words, cynical of authority figures and their big promises, and so Christian distinctness is essential to authentic witness.

I recall a phrase written in the bathroom of a student hostel. Above the hot-air hand-dryer were the words 'Press this button for a message from the Prime Minister'. It is a pretty good example of how many young people are increasingly cynical about the political process. It is nothing but hot air. Perhaps they feel the same about Christian leaders.

Christian witness has to combine the qualities which Paul expressed in 1 Thessalonians 1:5, 'Our gospel came to you not simply with words, but also with power, with the Holy Spirit and with deep conviction. You know how we lived among you for your sake.' Paul's description of the evangelistic task was not restricted to communicating information. He adds three other expressions: proclaimed in God's power, proclaimed with full conviction, and proclaimed with the Holy Spirit who empowered the preacher and pressed home the truth to the hearer. But there is a further phrase which is closely connected to the rest of the verse. Our gospel came to you with power, so 'you know how we lived among you for your sake'. It was this combination which made gospel communication so effective: God's Word, proclaimed in the power of the Spirit and demonstrated by – embodied in – the messenger himself. It is truth which produces godliness, as Paul said to Titus. Or, as New Testament theologian Tony Thistleton has expressed it, 'Purity of life constitutes part of the grammar of truth.'

This is exactly the burden of Jeremiah as he called the prophets of his day to be consistent in word and life. Not only had there been an appalling theological deterioration, but there had also been deep-set moral failure amongst the prophets. Instead of leading people away from sin, the prophets actually confirmed people in such activity. 'They live a lie,' he said. A true prophet will be one whose own life is an embodiment of the truth. A prophet's life is part of his message. In his helpful introduction to the story of Jeremiah, writer and preacher David Day expresses it like this: 'He is not like a postman who can do what he likes in private as long as he goes on delivering letters.'[4] Effective Christian ministry, authentic Christian ministry, is when Word, Spirit and life combine in what will be a genuine and consistent demonstration of God's character and purposes.

The resources we need

I suspect I know what you are thinking as you read this chapter, because it bothers me too. Paul's teaching seems unattainable. It is unrealistic. Thanks, but not me – I could not manage this. So we should notice something very significant: his strong call to distinct, holy living is surrounded by warm expressions concerning God's presence. As we have seen, he has used several Old Testament passages to underline that we belong to God and are redeemed, loved and empowered by him.

- Like Israel we have been brought out of exile, out of sin and death, and now we belong to a new family.
- We are God's dwelling place, his home; it is underlined with the expression 'I will live with them and walk among them' (6:16).
- We belong to a God who says, 'I will be a Father to you, and you will be my sons and daughters' (6:18).
- We are empowered by the Holy Spirit, who enables us to live as we should (6:6).

So the call to live our lives in conformity with God's standards is one which is accompanied by strong promises of his empowering presence and compassionate care. As we have already seen, Jesus is the 'Yes, the Amen' to all of God's promises which Paul has listed here. As Peter puts it in his second letter, these are great and precious promises: 'Through these . . . you may participate in the divine nature and escape the corruption in the world caused by evil desires' (2 Pet. 1:4).

Paul's teaching might have been aimed at the deterioration of Christian standards in the church in first-century Corinth, but his teaching in these verses is supremely relevant for Christian believers today. We face the constant temptation to compromise with the world. Its seductive appeal comes in many guises, and whether it is in the sphere of relationships, business, sexuality, materialism, ambition or lifestyle, we are under constant pressure to conform. But as God's holy temple, as God's children, as those empowered by God's Spirit, we should live lives that reflect the consistency and integrity of the Lord who calls us to follow him. In a cynical world, that is the kind of Christianity people need to see.

The Danish Christian Karen Blixen became well known for her book *Out of Africa*. She tells the story of working on her Kenyan coffee plantation and hiring a young servant named Kitau. One day he asked if she could write a letter of recommendation, because he wanted to leave and work for Sheik Ali in Mombasa. She said she would rather raise his pay than lose him, but he replied he had decided that he would be a Christian or a Muslim, but he was not yet sure which. So he had come to work for her for three months, to see the ways and habits of the Christians. Next he would go and work for Sheik Ali, and study the ways and habits of the Muslims. Then he would decide. Karen Blixen wrote that even a bishop would have said, as she said, 'Good God, Kitau, you might have told me that when you came here.'[5]

By contrast, Jennifer Rees Larcombe has written about her father, evangelist and conference speaker Tom Rees: 'I can honestly say that my father was exactly the same person when he was "off duty" with the family as he was when surrounded by admiring crowds. He showed me, rather than taught me, that integrity matters if you want to know God intimately.'[6]

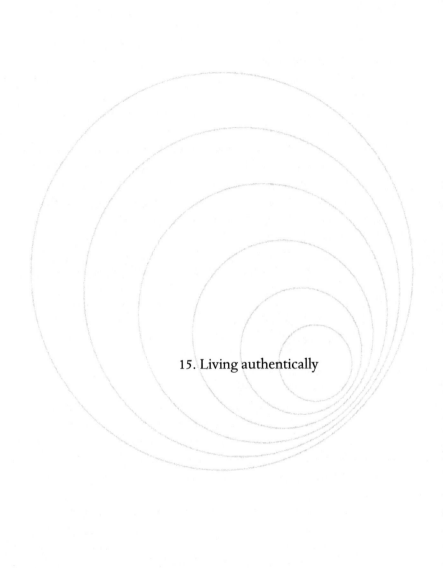

15. Living authentically

As a journalist, Martin Bell covered some very demanding war stories. Reflecting on the changes in journalism over the past thirty years, he suggests that 'we are entering the land of the inauthentic'. He argues that we live in an age of spin, an age of 'virtual news', where it is possible to enjoy a career as 'a virtual foreign correspondent without actually travelling very far or doing very much or taking any risks'. He tells of some journalists in Saigon who 'relied on valiant Vietnamese cameramen for the combat footage, while for their accompanying on-camera performances they would venture no further than the jungle foliage of the city's botanical gardens'.[1]

The Steven Spielberg movie *Catch Me if You Can* was based on the true story of the American conman who pocketed $2.5 million in the 1960s by forging cheques and taking on a variety of clever disguises. The movie's tagline was 'the true story of a real fake'. More recently in the UK, Youssef Babbou, posing variously as a golf partner of Bill Clinton, the boss of a chain of Las Vegas casinos and inventor of part of the space shuttle, managed to sustain a profligate lifestyle based on credit card fraud. The defence at his trial argued that he started the scams to cover medical costs for his daughter's heart operation, but the judge was unmoved, recommending that he be deported at the end of his twelve-year sentence.

We need not look only at the extreme examples. I live in a part of the world where cultivating the right image has become an art form. North Oxford is the home of academics, media moguls, business executives and other high-flyers. Sophisticated wine bars abound. Education is top of the agenda. Housing, clothing, children – all have the air of carefully understated sophistication. Yet most people, if they are honest, are hungry to discover what is real. In a world of spin, we are looking for something genuine. In a world of virtual experience, we want reality. In a world of image, we want substance.

One big advantage of experiencing weakness is that it helps us to see what is real. It is a wake-up call. We have already seen that 2 Corinthians 4 is at the heart of Paul's letter and is a profound expression of the true nature of the Christian faith. In contrast to the shoddy, cheap gospel of those in Corinth who promised health and wealth for all, Paul demonstrates that Christianity makes a difference not in our outward circumstances, but in our inward resources.

It enables us to see what is real. In the closing three verses of
2 Corinthians 4, he demonstrates how to live authentically.

> Therefore we do not lose heart. Though outwardly we are wasting
> away, yet inwardly we are being renewed day by day. For our light
> and momentary troubles are achieving for us an eternal glory that far
> outweighs them all. So we fix our eyes not on what is seen, but on
> what is unseen. For what is seen is temporary, but what is unseen is
> eternal. (4:16–18)

Paul gives three sets of contrasts which help us identify what really
matters.

Outward decline and inward renewal

We need hardly be reminded that our bodies are decaying, that
'outwardly we are wasting away' (4:16). Despite our best efforts, the
trend is irreversible. We may try jogging, aerobics, slimming, or hair
colouring, but we cannot halt the decay. We soon reach middle age,
when our broad mind and narrow waist change places. And although
the fastest-growing segment of our population in the UK is the group
who are over 100 (the 'robust elderly', they are called), we cannot halt
the steady decline. One day we will return to dust.

A professor of physics in New York has written:

> The search for eternal youth ... is with us even today. The baby boom
> generation, particularly with its emphasis on youth, seems determined
> to resist surrendering to Father Time, and has poured $40 billion into
> fuelling the current exercise and diet fads. Anyone who has ever stared
> in a mirror and watched the inexorable spread of wrinkles, sagging
> features, and greying hair has yearned for perpetual youth at some
> point ... No matter how rich, powerful, glamorous or influential
> you might be, to confront ageing is to confront the reality of your
> mortality.[2]

Perhaps for the first time Paul had begun to confront his own
mortality. We have already seen that he had frequently been close to
death in his missionary work, and having experienced the pressures
which this letter catalogues, perhaps he was beginning to conclude

that he would die before Christ returned. He had been carrying in his body the dying of Jesus. His present physical life felt vulnerable and frail. So it leads him to emphasize the renewing power of God to which he has already referred. In contrast to the deterioration he felt outwardly, the real Paul was being renewed day by day (4:16).

It is important to remember that we Christians live our lives in two dimensions at once. Paul is not describing a dualism, a body/soul dichotomy. He is helping us to see that our lives are in the overlap of two worlds. Our outer life is part of the mortality of the world around us. We live in this world and are vulnerable to pain and trouble like anybody else. But inwardly we participate in the world to come, the world of heaven, the world of glory. We have been born again inwardly by God's Spirit. Our inner life, our life in union with Christ, can keep fresh, increasing in power and vitality. In fact, Paul is continuing the theme of weakness and power. Our frailty as we grow older can be the occasion for an inner renewal by God's power.

This contrast is frequently seen in older people. As we grow older we can sometimes become sour and bitter, thinking only of selfish concerns as our horizons shrink. When I was a student I visited an eighty-year-old Christian each week. Living on his own, he expressed his gratitude to me for my friendship. But it was I who was the real beneficiary of the relationship, for to hear him describe his Christian faith, his hopes for heaven and his prayers for God's work world-wide was profoundly moving and deeply encouraging. His outward decline was obvious; but his inward renewal was a most impressive feature of the real Mr Perriam. He believed in the resurrection and he longed for heaven. To most outside observers, he lived an increasingly restricted life. But it was a truly authentic life. He knew what was real.

The inner renewal which Paul describes is not automatic, and the verse implies that we need to seek this day by day. We need to give at least as much attention to our inner life as we do to the care of our bodies and our outward appearance.

Present trouble and future glory

With what we might regard as surprising understatement, Paul describes his sufferings as 'light and momentary' (4:17). We have already seen that his sufferings were real, painful and extensive. But Christian suffering, however challenging, is only for this present life and, compared to everlasting glory, Paul implies that it is insignificant. He does more than contrast present suffering and future glory. He indicates that suffering 'achieves' something for the future. This needs to be linked with verse 18, where our sufferings encourage us to have the eternal perspective, fixing our eyes, our ambitions, our efforts, on the things that will last for ever.

When I was a school student I took part on several field courses as part of my studies in physical geography. On one occasion we had to climb a Welsh mountain called Cader Idris. Mountain climbing is not one of my ministries. It took a great deal of strenuous effort, as we encountered rise after rise. But the party leader sustained our spirits by urging us frequently to look at the peak, to keep our eyes on the destination. It was inspirational. It placed the inconveniences and discomfort of the climb in proper perspective. Paul frequently makes the link between suffering and glory. It is part of the theme he has already addressed: we experience both suffering and glory because of our unity with Christ.

We saw in chapter 10, when describing weakness and God's power, that troubles are an inevitable consequence of our fellowship with Christ. So in the same way, our union with Christ means that we are guaranteed a home in heaven, an eternal glory that 'far outweighs' our troubles (4:17). Paul has earlier described his pressures weighing down upon him. 'We were under great pressure, far beyond our ability to endure.' But from the perspective of eternity, such troubles are 'light'. Soon Paul will experience the 'weight' of God's glory. His troubles are 'momentary'; his experience of glory will be 'eternal'.

It is precisely this perspective which leads to authentic living. For it puts us in touch with the real world, not the world which is passing away. This way of thinking and living will make us more truly human, not less so. Tom Wright has a very helpful illustration. 'We sometimes speak of somebody who has been sick being "just a shadow of their former self". But what Paul seems to be saying here is that human beings are just a shadow of their *future* selves ... Everything that humans, at their deepest and best moments, are reaching out for, struggling after, longing for, and dreaming of, will finally be fulfilled.'[3]

The seen and the unseen

> So we fix our eyes not on what is seen, but on what is unseen. For
> what is seen is temporary, but what is unseen is eternal. (4:18)

Robert Green writes: 'Everything is judged by its appearance; what is
unseen counts for nothing. Never let yourself get lost in the crowd,
then, or buried in oblivion. Stand out. Be conspicuous, at all costs.
Make yourself a magnet of attention by appearing larger, more
colourful, more mysterious than the bland and timid masses.'[4]

Our world places great emphasis on treasure on earth rather than
treasure in heaven, and it is not easy for Christians to think differently.
For many people around us, the prevailing philosophy is 'eat, drink
and watch telly, for tomorrow we diet'. They are concerned only to
maximize on their present experience. As far as most of our
contemporaries are concerned, all religions are mocked by the hard,
white smile of the skull. So now is the time to accumulate, now is the
time to enjoy. For Christians to think differently, a radical change of
perspective is called for. This is only possible as we fix our eyes not on
what is seen, but on what is unseen (4:18).

Paul has argued that this is the perspective the Corinthians lacked.
For a display-conscious Corinth, Paul needed to call them to change
their outlook, to have the perspective of faith.

- 'You are looking only on the surface of things.' (10:7)
- 'We live by faith, not by sight.' (5:7)
- 'So that you can answer those who take pride in what is seen
  rather than in what is in the heart.' (5:12)

Jesus explained in the Beatitudes that his values were not of this world.
He had crept into life's window and swapped the price tags round, so
that those things which were of great value were now of little value,
and those things which were of little value were now of great value.
Learning to value the unseen, the eternal, is part of our Christian
discipleship, and Paul explains that our troubles will help us to do this.
They help us to see that this world, and our physical bodies, are
decaying as a result of sin, and that what really matters is inner
renewal and eternal glory.

It is a paradox, of course: looking at what you cannot see. We must be careful once again to avoid any suggestion that he is contrasting the physical and the spiritual, as if waiting to be released from the evil material body to enjoy the freedom of floating on a cloud. No, the contrast is between the present and the future, for he makes it clear in the next chapter that he will one day have this 'tent' replaced with 'a building from God, an eternal house in heaven' (5:1–5). Paul's teaching on the resurrection points to the fact that our future bodies will not be subject to corruption and decay. Just as our bodies are presently wearing out, the same is also true of the created order. We will one day enjoy the true existence for which God is presently preparing us. It is this world which is a shadow; the real world is the world for which we are heading.

In the world's estimation, Paul was a failure. He was converted in the course of a brilliant career, yet he tells us in Philippians that he counted those things of little worth. All of his work, his suffering, journeys and hardships would have looked foolish. But Paul's estimate was different; he used a different accounting system. So it should be for us. You may know some Christians who have not got the job they wanted because they follow Christ; or the partner they would have liked to marry; or the material resources that their peers might have. But they have a different value system. They know that one day they will experience something that will make all the things this world considers of value look utterly worthless.

Graham Staines was an Australian missionary working amongst people with leprosy and tribal peoples in Orissa, North India. On 22 January 1999 he was brutally murdered outside a church, along with his two sons. Around the world Christian and non-Christian alike were outraged at such an atrocity. But his grieving widow, Gladys Staines, told a newspaper reporter the following day, 'I'm deeply upset but I'm not angry, for Jesus has taught us how to love our enemies.' She chose to stay and continue her husband's work, to suffer joyfully in serving Christ. Her words were carried in national dailies across India and beyond. As a result, hundreds if not thousands of Hindus came to Christians to ask for Bibles to read, and many asked the question, 'Why are you Christians different?'

How might we evaluate such a tragedy? Wasted lives? A foolish investment? My friend Vinoth Ramachandra, working in South Asia, said not long after the event that he could not help feeling that a middle-aged Australian widow had done more for the cause of the gospel in India than all the slick evangelists and 24-hour channel networks now beaming into that country.

Paul has demonstrated that the power of the gospel is seen through the weakness of the crucified Jesus and through the frailty of his followers. In the light of Christ's death and resurrection, and our union with him, our lives have been transformed. We live in anticipation of the reality of eternity. We fix our eyes on:

- inward renewal, not outward decline;
- future glory, not present trouble;
- the unseen realities of our future home, not the temporary glitter of this world.

To have this perspective is truly to live authentically.

Section E – Over to you...

- What are the particular circumstances which create frustration or stress in your life, and in what ways can you bring these more consciously into God's presence and under his sovereign care?
- In our culture there are many things which contaminate us as Christian believers, and for most of us this includes the pervasive influence of liberal sexual attitudes and behaviour. How can you guard your heart and mind, and remain faithful to God in the particular pressures which you face?
- The call to Christian distinctness is not a call for withdrawal from the world where God has placed us. In what areas of life will Christian saltiness be most evident for you?
- In what ways does your Christian service sometimes seem to be more about image than substance?
- What are the unseen things which motivate you to live in the light of eternity?

Postscript

I am God Almighty; walk before me and be blameless.' (Gen. 17:1)

In his essay entitled 'God and Me', A. L. Kennedy refers to 'that vague intimation of being watched, of a presence beyond imagining standing much too close behind you with something unnerving in mind'.[1] In chapter 1 we heard the Lord's call to Abram to walk with integrity beneath God's watching eye. Throughout this book we have seen that Paul was able to affirm repeatedly that each area of his Christian service was carried out in God's presence, with God as his witness. His life was lived in the sight of God.

There is the possibility, hinted at by A. L. Kennedy, that the awareness of God's all-seeing presence could induce fear or paralysis. Certainly we have seen that leading with God watching encourages us not to underestimate our moral obligations, not to live casually or carelessly, but to walk in a way worthy of the God who has called us. But perhaps we should not conclude without remembering that, for forgiven sinners, the Lord's presence evokes not fear but comfort, not cringing shame but liberating joy, not paralysis but energetic service.

One of the many wonderful privileges of being his dearly loved children is that his presence sustains and supports us throughout our journey. By his Spirit he is with us, alongside us, empowering, guiding and comforting us.

We need to hear this in its simplicity, for the biblical call to integrity is demanding, and we might have reached the end of this book acutely aware of our need of God's grace. So let us encourage one another with that most profound thought: *God is with us*. The God who sees is the God who cares and provides, the God who supports and empowers.

David was a man of integrity, but he knew a great deal about both failure and forgiveness. In the midst of a grateful testimony to God's forgiving grace, the Lord speaks to David. 'I will instruct you and teach you in the way you should go. I will counsel you and watch over you' (Ps. 32:8). Through the centuries God's people have taken this promise as their own. He is the God who *watches over us*. If you have ever seen a child taking its first steps, you might have noticed the behaviour of the parents. They are alongside, carefully watching, ready to support, guiding and protecting. Like David, we know that the Lord is with us, leading and teaching, with his eye upon us. When Moses appealed to God for his help and guidance, the Lord replied, 'My presence will go with you and I will give you rest.' That is the special security that every disciple knows.

He is watching, but he is no neutral observer. His eye is upon us and his arms are around us. His Spirit is alongside us and within us, empowering and transforming us.

C. S. Lewis wrote about this many years ago in his classic book *Mere Christianity*.

> You see what is happening. The Christ himself, the Son of God who is man (just like you) and God (just like his Father) is actually at your side and is already at that moment beginning to turn your pretence into a reality ... The real Son of God is at your side. He is beginning to turn you into the same thing as himself. He is beginning, so to speak, to 'inject' His kind of life and thought ... into you.[2]

As for Paul, the closing words of his life – the final paragraph of his apostolic writing – was devoted to exactly this truth. Imprisoned in Rome, threatened with execution, cold, vulnerable and with no human support, he writes: 'But the Lord stood at my side and gave me strength' (2 Tim. 4:17). Paul had known this throughout his life. He had carried out his ministry in the sight of God, leading with God watching, serving 'before God'. But that meant God's sustaining and empowering presence, right to the end of his life as an old man now in a dark dungeon. The Lord stood with him and strengthened him.

Leading with God watching means serving with God providing.

The way in which he does so is enormously varied. Here are some of the ways in which we know his provision, enabling us to live with integrity. It is a closing checklist, and I invite you to reflect on whether these resources are truly being made your own.

- *Remember God's call*: we are able to cope with the ups and downs of Christian service when we are sure of who it is who has called us, and what it is he has called us to do. We have seen that, by God's mercy, he equips us for service and invites us to walk in a way that is worthy of that holy calling.
- *Practise God's presence*: our calling is to walk blamelessly before him, and an awareness of God's watching eye and sustaining presence is fundamental to a life of integrity. Nurturing our fellowship with him, practising his presence and knowing the Spirit's empowering are essential ingredients in a daily life of integrity.
- *Receive God's Word*: the truth of Scripture sets us free, enabling us to live as we should in each area of life. Committing ourselves to study, apply and live the truth is the only recipe for renewed minds and transformed behaviour.
- *Rely on God's people*: integrity is nurtured in Christian community, and most particularly through relationships of support and accountability. Identifying a small group of friends who can serve us in this way is a vital support on the journey.
- *Rest on God's grace*: as James reminds us, we all stumble in many ways, yet our calling to walk blamelessly is set in the context of God's work in Jesus Christ. It is not through our best efforts, for our justification is by faith alone, in Christ alone, through grace alone. In every situation of pressure we may experience the reality of the super-abundant grace of our Lord poured upon us, along with the faith and love which are in Christ Jesus (1 Tim. 1:14).

Since through God's mercy we have this ministry, 'we do not lose heart' (2 Cor. 4:1). We should 'never tire of doing what is right' (2 Thess. 3:13). We serve in the presence of the Lord who says to us, 'My grace is sufficient for you, for my power is made perfect in weakness' (2 Cor. 12:9). And with all God's people we take up Paul's closing encouragement to the Corinthians: 'May the grace of the Lord Jesus Christ, and the love of God, and the fellowship of the Holy Spirit be with you all' (2 Cor. 13:14).

For further reading

I have found the following resources helpful in my research for this book.

Paul Barnett, *The Second Epistle to the Corinthians*, The New International Commentary in the New Testament (Eerdmans, 1997).

Paul Barnett, *The Message of 2 Corinthians*, The Bible Speaks Today (IVP, 1988).

Donald A. Carson, *From Triumphalism to Maturity* (Baker, 1984).

Roy Clements, *The Strength of Weakness* (Christian Focus Publications, 1994).

Scott J. Hafemann, *The NIV Application Commentary, 2 Corinthians* (Zondervan, 2000).

David Prior, *The Suffering and the Glory* (Hodder & Stoughton, 1985).

Michael B. Thompson, *Transforming Grace* (The Bible Reading Fellowship, 1998).

Notes

Foreword
1. John Poulton, *A Today Sort of Evangelism* (Lutterworth, 1977), pp. 60–61, 79.

1. Why integrity matters
1. Donald A. Carson, *A Call to Spiritual Reformation* (IVP, 1992), p. 14.
2. Quoted in Bryan Chappell, *Christ-Centred Preaching* (Baker, 2005), p. 209.
3. Richard Higginson, *Transforming Leadership* (SPCK, 1996), p. 53.
4. Margaret Thorsborne, *The Seven Heavenly Virtues of Leadership*, Management Today series (Australian Institute of Management, 2003).
5. See Eph. 4:1; Phil. 1:27; Col. 1:10.
6. Max DePree, *Leadership Jazz* (Doubleday, 1992), pp. 1–3, quoted in Walter C. Wright, *Relational Leadership* (Paternoster Press, 2000), pp. 117, 118.

2. What integrity looks like
1. Ben Lewis, 'Hammer & Tickle', *Prospect* magazine, May 2006.
2. *The Independent*, 29 May 2006.
3. Thorsborne, *Seven Heavenly Virtues*.

3. True accountability
1. Rosie Millard, *New Statesman*, 13 February 2006.
2. Richard Reeves, 'Should the state "do" God?', *New Statesman*, 10 April 2006.
3. Peter Brain, *Going the Distance* (Matthias Media, 2004), p. 119.

4. Serving others
1. Kent and Barbara Hughes, *Liberating Ministry from the Success Syndrome* (Tyndale House Publishers, 1987), p. 48.
2. See Jude 12; Ezek. 34:1–10.
3. John R. W. Stott, *The Message of Acts*, The Bible Speaks Today (IVP, 1990), p. 329.
4. Colin Morris, *The Word and the Words* (Epworth, 1975), pp. 34–35.

5. Gospel priorities

1. John Pilger, 'The real first casualty of war', *New Statesman*, 24 April 2006.
2. Ajith Fernando, *Jesus Driven Ministry* (IVP, 2002).

7. Building community

1. See Rom. 1:11–12; 14:19; 1 Cor. 14:3–5, 12, 17; Eph. 4:12–13.
2. Daniel Goleman, *The New Leaders* (Little, Brown, 2002), p. 47.
3. Clive Mather, Temple Address, London, 17 October 2004.
4. Paul's reference in this verse may be deliberately targeted at the false teachers who 'corrupted Corinthian minds away from pure devotion to Christ (11:3)', Paul Barnett, '2 Corinthians', *The New International Commentary on the New Testament* (Eerdmans, 1997), p. 360.
5. Max DePree, *Leadership is an Art* (Dell Publishing, 1989), p. 11.
6. Brain, *Going the Distance*, p. 145.
7. *The Times*, 8 April 2006.

8. Confronting failure

1. Paul Beasley-Murray, *A Call to Excellence* (Hodder & Stoughton, 1995), p. 56.
2. Ben Witherington III, *Conflict and Community in Corinth* (Eerdmans, 1995), p. 328.
3. Quoted in Brain, *Going the Distance*, p. 83.
4. Tom Wright, *Paul for Everyone, 2 Corinthians* (SPCK, 2003), pp. 18–19.
5. Issiaka Coulbalu, *Africa Bible Commentary* (Word Alive/Zondervan, 2006).
6. Brain, *Going the Distance*, p. 95.
7. Walter Wright, *Relational Leadership* (Paternoster Press, 2000), p. 202.
8. Michael Griffiths, *Discovering 1 and 2 Timothy*, Crossway Bible Guide (Crossway, 1996), p. 215.

9. Handling money

1. F. F. Bruce, *The Pauline Circle* (Paternoster Press, 1985), pp. 39, 62, 63.

10. Weakness and power

1. John R. W. Stott, *Calling Christian Leaders* (IVP, 2002), p. 58.
2. David Smith, *Against the Stream* (IVP, 2003), p. 92.

3. In reading the Servant Songs I have benefited from the commentary on Isaiah by Derek Thomas, *God Delivers*, Welwyn Commentaries (Evangelical Press, 1991).

4. Tom Wright, *Reflecting the Glory* (The Bible Reading Fellowship, 1997), p. 36.

5. Robert Greene, *The 48 Laws of Power* (Profile Books, 2002), p. 2.

11. Status and true ambition

1. Gordon MacDonald, *Restoring Your Spiritual Passion* (Highland Books, 1987), pp. 98–99.

2. Alain de Botton, *Status Anxiety* (Penguin, 2005), pp. 3–4.

3. Jo Owen, *How to Lead* (Pearson Education, 2005), p. 192.

4. Eugene Peterson, *The Gift, Reflections on Christian Ministry* (Marshall Pickering, 1995), p. 17.

5. These verses are something of a challenge, and I am indebted to various commentaries for assistance, including Scott Hafeman, *2 Corinthians*, NIV Application Commentary (Zondervan, 2000).

6. J. I. Packer, *A Passion for Faithfulness* (Hodder & Stoughton, 1995), p. 209.

12. Pride and the call to humility

1. Eugene Peterson, *Under the Unpredictable Plant* (Eerdmans, 1992), p. 113.

2. See Galatians 4:13–15; 6:11.

3. Helmut Thielicke, *The Prayer that Spans the World* (James Clarke, 1960), p. 28.

4. Michael Ramsay, *The Christian Priest Today* (SPCK, 1985), quoted in Beasley-Murray, *A Call to Excellence*, p. 213.

14. Living consistently

1. Dallas Willard, *Renovation of the Heart* (IVP, 2002), p. 21.

2. John White, *The Fight* (IVP, 1977), p. 179.

3. Donald McCullough, *The Trivialization of God* (Navpress, 1995, pp. 14–18), quoted in Peter Lewis, *The Message of the Living God* (IVP, 2000), pp. 320–321.

4. David Day, *Jeremiah: Speaking for God in a Time of Crisis* (IVP, 1987), p. 89.

5. Karen Blixen, *Out of Africa* (Penguin, 1954, reprinted 1984), p. 47.

6. Jennifer Rees Larcombe, *Journey into God's Heart* (Hodder & Stoughton, 2006), p. 29.

15. Living authentically

1. Martin Bell, *The Gates of Fire* (Phoenix, 2003), p. 183.
2. Professor Kaku, *Visions* (OUP, 1998), pp. 200–201.
3. Wright, *Reflecting the Glory*, pp. 41–42.
4. Green, 'Law 6, Court attention at all costs', *The 48 Laws of Power*, p. 21.

Postscript

1. A. L. Kennedy, 'God and Me', *Granta*, vol. 93, Spring 2006, p. 82.
2. C. S. Lewis, *Mere Christianity* (Collins, 1952), p. 158.